P9-DEW-036

CRAZY FISH

All the kids started saying it. "Oh, hoo ha! There's Crazy Fish!"

Mrs. Fish heard them. I know she did. But she just smiled and picked up a wad of paper from the floor. She tossed the paper into her can with a flip of her wrist. Then, just as if it was part of her cleaning job, she twirled around. She was dancing for the kids! Everyone was laughing and calling. Some girls clapped their hands in time to her dancing.

I stood there, staring at her. My face was burning. I hated her. I didn't even know her, and I hated her! She was making a fool of herself. My fists clenched. "Stop it," I said. "Stop it. Stop it!"

Other Avon Flare Books by
Norma Fox Mazer

AFTER THE RAIN
DOWNTOWN
SILVER
TAKING TERRI MUELLER

Avon Books are available at special quantity discounts for bulk purchases for sales promotions, premiums, fund raising or educational use. Special books, or book excerpts, can also be created to fit specific needs.

For details write or telephone the office of the Director of Special Markets, Avon Books, Dept. FP, 1350 Avenue of the Americas, New York, New York 10019, 1-800-238-0658.

MRS. FISH, APE, AND ME, THE DUMP QUEEN

Norma Fox Mazer

AN AVON FLARE BOOK

If you purchased this book without a cover, you should be aware that this book is stolen property. It was reported as "unsold and destroyed" to the publisher, and neither the author nor the publisher has received any payment for this "stripped book."

AVON BOOKS
A division of
The Hearst Corporation
1350 Avenue of the Americas
New York, New York 10019

Copyright © 1980 by Norma Fox Mazer
Text Designer: Claire Counihan
Published by arrangement with E. P. Dutton
a Division of Elsevier-Dutton Publishing Company, Inc.
Library of Congress Catalog Card Number: 79-20262
ISBN: 0-380-69153-1

All rights reserved, which includes the right to reproduce this book or portions thereof in any form whatsoever except as provided by the U.S. Copyright Law. For information address E. P. Dutton, a Division of Elsevier-Dutton Publishing Company, Inc. 2 Park Avenue, New York, New York 10016.

First Avon Camelot Printing: January 1982
First Avon Flare Printing: November 1984

AVON FLARE BOOKS TRADEMARK REG. U.S. PAT. OFF. AND IN OTHER COUNTRIES, MARCA REGISTRADA, HECHO EN CANADA.

Printed in Canada

UNV 10 9 8 7

MRS. FISH, APE, AND ME, THE DUMP QUEEN

At Home in the Dump

"Old Dad," I said, "if I didn't go to school, I could help you every day in the dump." Old Dad didn't say anything. "You listening? I *said*, If I didn't go to school—"

He put down his coffee cup. "Heard you," he growled. His voice was always growly, as if he had thorns in his throat. "You go to school, Joyce."

"Give me one good reason," I said. I hated school. It was starting again in four days. All summer I'd been happy with Old Dad.

"Same reason I told you last year, and year before, and year before that," he said. "You learn everything you can, Joyce. You go there and *learn*." He took his keys from the nail by the door. "You coming?"

We walked on our private road through the field, down the hill, and through the woods to the dump. People thought because we ran the dump and lived *near* the dump, that we lived *in* it. We couldn't even *see* the dump from our house!

It was a cool sunny day, and the wind sounded nice in

the trees. Saturday was our busiest day. When we got to the dump Old Dad opened up the work shack, and I ran down the road to unlock the chain.

There were oak and pine trees along the road, and lots of sumac. All summer there were wildflowers along the edge of the road—blue sailor, daisies, king devil, and bug-loss. Now fall was coming, and there were goldenrod and asters.

I knew everything about our road. I knew the animals that lived near it—red squirrels, woodchucks, chipmunks, and a skunk family. Once when there was snow on the ground I found a big orange-and-black butterfly frozen into one of the ruts. I took it home and warmed it up. It came back to life and I let it go. Old Dad said it would go to Mexico for the winter.

When I got to the gate it wasn't seven o'clock yet, which was our opening time, but already people had dumped their big plastic bags of garbage outside the chain. Some people dumped their garbage there even when we were open.

Old Dad's sign was tacked right to a tree by the side of the gate where everybody could see it.

QUEENSHIP TOWN DUMP.
HOURS 7am-5pm Mon.-Sat. Closed Sun.
RULES. NO GARBAGE DUMPING AT GATE.
DON'T PUT FOOD GARBAGE WITH OTHER STUFF.
DRIVE SLOW INTO DUMP. *THIS MEANS YOU!*

I walked back down the road. I was whistling. Near the dump a car went rattling past. I heard Old Dad working on the dozer. When you came to the dump, first you saw a big open sandy place that almost looked like a beach. No flies, no smell, hardly any garbage around. Old Dad's dump was special, because of the way he took care of things.

Food garbage—meat bones, eggshells, banana peels, rotten tomatoes—went in just one place in the ravine in back of the dump. Every day Old Dad buried all that stuff under fresh earth. The garbage started changing because of the bacteria in the earth. It broke down, and pretty soon it wasn't garbage anymore. It was nice, beautiful rich soil.

In the spring when we made our garden by our house, Old Dad always brought a load of earth from the garbage pit. It was the best soil. It made our vegetables and flowers grow. Our sunflowers were eight feet tall; we grew huge juicy tomatoes, green peppers that shone like glass, and lettuce, turnips, potatoes, cucumbers, and anything else we wanted. Anything would grow in our garden. We also had an asparagus patch, rhubarb, and a strawberry bed.

Besides the pit for fresh garbage, Old Dad had special places for everything else. There were open sheds where he worked on stuff that could be fixed up. Anybody who wanted something Old Dad had fixed only had to ask. Refrigerators, TVs, and washing machines never stayed around long.

Right behind Old Dad's work shack we piled up metal—tin from barn roofs, copper wiring, aluminum cans, and cast-iron radiators. Near the metal was a bin for magazines and newspapers, and another bin for rags. When we collected enough rags, paper, and metal, we loaded our pickup truck and drove into town to Olsen and Farson Junk Dealers.

People brought all sorts of stuff to our dump. Most of it was junky, but lots of it was still good: stoves, dryers, couches, beds, typewriters, mattresses, books, and toys.

Toys made a whole list of their own—balls, bikes, skateboards, games, dolls, and guns.

There were pots with holes in them, pans without handles, glasses, jars, dishes, clothes, shoes and boots, curtains, radios by the dozen, lamps, tables, trunks, cribs, pictures and paintings, vacuum cleaners, sewing machines, plants, thermoses, skis and sleds, jars of pills and bottles of medicine, eyeglasses, and oh . . . everything. I never understood it. People spent all that money, and then they threw their things away.

All morning, cars and pickup trucks poured into the dump. In and out, in and out. I was on the baby dozer behind Old Dad, standing up, my hands on his shoulders. We pushed sand from the sand bank into the fresh garbage pit. One minute flies and smells, then just as quick as the dirt covered the garbage they were gone.

A station wagon drove in. The lady behind the wheel tapped the horn. I recognized RB Byrd and his mother and sister. "You go," Old Dad said, stopping the dozer so I could jump off.

Mrs. Byrd pulled a big stack of newspapers to the back of the wagon. I tossed them to one side. RB poked his sister Bubba and pointed to Old Dad. "Ape Man," he whispered. I wanted to kill him. I knew how Old Dad looked. He was short with short legs and long arms, and sort of sloping shoulders. He was very strong, and when he walked he swung his arms and had a sort of bowlegged swagger. I liked the way he looked. I liked his little blue eyes and big thick bristly white eyebrows.

I threw the last bag of Byrd garbage into the pit. I heard their car drive away. Good riddance to bad garbage!

Later in the afternoon so many cars were in the dump they got jammed up. People dumped their garbage in all the wrong places. Nobody paid any attention to Old Dad's rules. They couldn't wait. They threw the stuff out of their cars and drove away.

Old Dad started shouting. "Hey, you! Come back! Screwballs! Jerks! Don't you know how to read signs?"

Around four-thirty things started to quiet down. "Joyce," Old Dad called, "bottle." I was stacking wood. Old Dad handed me a little bottle. I spit on it and wiped a patch of glass clean. It was a dark blue-green. "Good one, Old Dad," I said, pocketing it. I collected bottles. In my room I had a shelf full—no special kinds, just any bottles I liked.

We worked until five o'clock. "Closin' time!" Old Dad yelled. "Closin' time!" As soon as the last car was gone, I ran down the road and put up the chain. Then we went back to our house and washed, and changed out of our work clothes. For supper we had tomatoes from our garden, fried chicken, bread, milk for me, and coffee for Old Dad. Old Dad ate without talking. I didn't say anything, either. I was thinking just one thing. *Four more days until school starts*. I finished supper and washed my dishes. *Four more days . . . four more days. . . .* That's what I kept thinking. And I felt so bad.

❧ 2 ❧

Orange Peel in Her Ear

There was a story I told myself at night about my mother. *First there's her car traveling down a road in wintertime. Suddenly all these cars smash up. My mother gets out of her cracked-up car and walks away. Nobody sees her. She's very confused. She says, "Where am I?" She has amnesia and doesn't remember her name is Joyce, or that she has a daughter with the same name.*

She goes someplace and is living there and is always wondering who she really is. One day she bumps her head and everything comes back to her. She remembers that she's Joyce Adams and she has a daughter that she left with her brother, Henry Adams. Right away, she comes here, and we laugh and kiss and hug and cry. Then my mother decides to stay with Old Dad and me, and we're just like a real family.

The last time I saw my mother I was four years old. I was carrying my rag doll, Mama Big Joyce Doll, which had been my mother's when she was a little girl. It was winter, and the snow was like a giant cake on top of Old Dad's house. My mother was leaving me for a few weeks while she went down to Florida to look for a job. She

6

knew her brother would take good care of me. As soon as she had a job, she'd send for me.

My mother never got to Florida. She only got as far as a town called Shoemakersville, in Pennsylvania. That was where her car was in the accident with about five other cars.

Old Dad said my mother was pretty, and that I looked like her. I wasn't so sure. I thought if my mother was here she'd comb my hair in the morning and ask me questions about school, and maybe she'd tell me I was pretty.

Old Dad never said stuff like that. I didn't mind. He was Old Dad, and that was the way he was. He didn't say too much, but sometimes he'd tell me stories about when he was a boy, and about my mother, and all that.

Ever since he was a small child, he told me, he got up earlier than anyone else. He got up with the sun in the summer, and before the sun in the winter. I always wanted to get up when he did, but most of the time I slept too late.

The first day of school I dressed very fast because I heard Old Dad downstairs. I slept upstairs in the attic. There was an east-facing window right by my bed. The window was in two pieces. The bottom part was plain glass, but the top was colored glass, little pieces of blue and gold and green glass that lit up and shone all over the wall when the sun came through them in the morning.

I stuffed my nightgown under my pillow and kissed Mama Big Joyce Doll, who always slept with me.

"Hello, Old Dad," I said, going down the stairs. I sat on the bottom step to tie my sneakers. "How come you're still here?" It was almost seven-thirty.

"Been out," he said. "Came back for a cup of coffee."

I kissed his head. "Came back to see me because it's the first day of school."

"Eat your cereal."

I filled my dish from the pot on the stove and sat down at the table. "Wish I didn't have to go."

"You have to go."

"Why?"

"Don't start that stuff, Joyce. You go, and you learn. You want to be a dumbbell?"

"I'm not a dumbbell."

"Will be if you don't go to school."

I made a hole in the oatmeal and poured in milk. I wouldn't want to be called DUMB along with everything else.

Way back when I first started school I *was* dumb. One time I went home with another girl, Noreen Norris. Noreen's mother said to me, "Where do you live, Joyce?" And I said, "In the dump, Mrs. Norris." Mrs. Norris laughed. "Oh, Joyce, that's not a very nice thing to say about your home!" I was bewildered. I didn't know *dump* was a bad word. To me, dump was home.

That first year in school I woke up with a stomachache every morning. Sometimes Old Dad would let me stay home, but mostly he said I had to go to school.

Noreen had told everyone I lived in the dump, and at recess and out in the playground no one played with me. Sometimes I watched the other kids play. They looked like they were having so much fun. Other times I just walked around singing to myself, glad no one was noticing me, because when they did they shouted things.

Dirty Joyce, lives in a dump, dirty dump, dirty dump, dirty dump. She smells like a rat; she eats dead cat!

"Do people ever eat cats?" I asked Old Dad.

"Might eat anything if you got hungry enough," he said. "Finish your cereal."

"Did you ever eat a cat?"

Old Dad looked at the clock on the wall. It was round and red with gold curlicues all along the edges. We saved it from the dump. It kept good time, even though it made a noise, sort of like a chicken gurgling.

"You walking down with me?" Old Dad said. He washed his cup and took his brown work jacket from a peg on the wall.

I got my new notebook and pencils for school. I was wearing one of my new blouses and my blue-and-white sneakers. Old Dad and I walked down the hill and through the woods. "You didn't answer my question," I said.

Old Dad pretended he didn't hear me. But I saw him smiling. His mouth was just lifting up a little bit, in a special way. Maybe somebody else couldn't tell it was a smile, but I could.

"Well?" I said.

"Well, what?"

"You ever eat a cat?"

"Huh! Done plenty of things in my time, but I never ate no cat."

"Then I guess people don't eat them," I said.

At the dump Old Dad went toward the work shack and I went down to the main road. First thing, I looked in our mailbox. It was silver and made like a little house with a peaked red roof. We used to have an old plain one, until someone threw this one out and Old Dad saved it.

In case anybody wanted to send mail to the dump, Old Dad had painted QUEENSHIP TOWN DUMP on the side, and below that, our name, ADAMS. I peered in, and my heart jumped the way it always did. Even though I knew better, I thought, *Maybe today. Maybe today there'll be a letter from my mother.*

Sharon Mason was waiting at the school bus stop with a little boy. Sharon Mason was very high-class. She lived on Kentwood Road in a blue house with two statues of brown deer on the lawn.

"Who's that?" the boy said. He was wearing a red shirt and carrying a little briefcase. I could tell he was high-class, too. His name was stitched in white down one arm of his shirt. S-T-E-V-E-N.

"Who's what?" Sharon said.

"Her." Steven looked at me. I smiled at him.

"Oh, her. That's Joyce." Sharon pushed his head around so he wouldn't see me. She bent over and whispered to him. *Bzzz, bzzz, bzzz.* Whisper, whisper, whisper. Giggle, giggle, giggle. Bet I know what she's whispering. *Joyce lives in the dump.* Who cares? Not me. I heard that stuff enough times. Sticks and stones will break my bones, but words will never harm me. Say anything you want, Sharon, you don't have to whisper it.

I started whistling. This was the worst time of the day, just waiting for the school bus with home so close, and knowing I couldn't go back there.

The next-worst time was riding the school bus with Sharon Mason and her best friend, Linda Justice, and RB Byrd, and all of them. I looked out the window all the way.

We had a new teacher. He had a long mustache that drooped down around his mouth. He sat on the edge of his desk swinging his legs. "Class, my name is Donald LaSorta. Let's get to know each other." He looked right at me. "You, the girl with the yellow hair. What's your name?"

"Joyce," I said.

"Joyce what?" He smiled at me.

"Joyce Adams." I liked him, but I wished he would pick someone else first. Now everyone would notice me.

"Think you're going to like my class, Joyce?"

Everybody giggled. They always laughed when I answered questions. Mr. LaSorta looked around. "Someone going to share the joke with me?" Then he forgot me and asked other people their names.

After that, we did all the usual stuff. We got seats. We got geography books, and math books. We got our gym and music schedule. We had announcements from Mr. Reicher, the principal. Then it was lunchtime. And then the afternoon was going past. I kept looking at the clock and thinking how many hours, and how many half-hours, and how many minutes, and even how many seconds till I would be home again.

Pretty soon it was only fifteen minutes until dismissal. Mr. LaSorta sat on his desk, swinging his legs. "Class, we'll have fifteen minutes of poetry."

"Poetry!" someone groaned.

"We'll be doing this every once in a while," Mr. LaSorta said. "And I bet you'll even like it."

"Oh, no," someone else said. "Nev-ver!"

Mr. LaSorta smiled. He didn't get mad the way some teachers did when you talked. "Poetry isn't just rhymes like, 'The mouse lives in a house.' And it's not words you can't understand. Poetry has to do with words, and with music, and with rhythm."

Then he looked at me first again. "Joyce, can you tell me some words you think are poetry?"

I said, "Good morning." I didn't know why I said it!

Everyone laughed. My face got hot. "You know," Mr. LaSorta said, "I never thought of it, but I think you're right. That *is* poetry. Good morning. Good evening. Good-bye. Those common expressions have something special. They reverberate. They have music, they make you feel."

I wished he would stop talking about it. I wished he would look at someone else. I was glad when RB Byrd waved his hand in the air.

"Mr. LaSorta," RB said, "I know a poem. I just made up a poem."

"Terrific! Share it with us."

RB Byrd looked at me out of the corner of his eyes. "I know a girl," he recited, "who has an orange peel in her ear." He choked, laughing. "Do you hear? *Orange peel* in her ear. Yeeech! She—smells—queer!"

RB sat down. The whole class was laughing. Kids were poking each other and saying, "Orange peel in her *ear*!"

I sat still. I didn't move at all. I looked straight ahead. I remembered how, a long time ago, I would go home crying. And Old Dad would say, *Okay to cry, but don't let them see you.* My neck felt stiff. But after a few minutes the queer hot feeling in my eyes went away.

Everybody was making so much noise that Mr. LaSorta banged on his desk. "All right, all right!"

The bell rang. Everyone ran for their lockers. I got my stuff and went outside to wait for the bus. I was the first one on. I looked out the window all the way home. And all the way home, in my head I recited RB's poem. I didn't want to. But I did.

3

Ape Man

Friday in the cafeteria I saw a girl sitting alone at the table next to mine. There was nobody at my table either. The girl had brown eyes and long straight brown hair with bangs. Her teeth stuck out a little in front. She was looking around and smiling at everyone. I could tell that she was new because no one was sitting with her.

She looked over at me. "Hi," she said. "You waiting for somebody?" I shook my head.

She took her lunch and moved to my table. "Want company?" she said. "I do!" She sat down. "I hate eating alone, don't you?"

"I don't mind," I said.

"What's your name? My name is Lacey Laurence."

"Joyce Adams." I unwrapped my sandwich. My face was hot. What did she want?

"I'm new here," she said.

"I know."

"Oh, boy, I just hope I'm going to like it here," she said. "I loved it at my old school! I cried for three days when my mom and dad told me we had to move."

She was eating something out of a pink plastic cup. "This is *won*-derful," she said. "It's my mom's beef stew. Want a bite?" She held out her spoon to me. I shook my head. I didn't know what to say. First I thought it was a trick, her sitting down with me. Then I knew it couldn't be, because she was new.

"You don't talk much," she said.

"My Old Dad says, Just talk when you have something to say."

"Oh, boy, I bet your Old Dad wouldn't like me, then! I talk all the time. Am I boring you? Am I rattling on too much? My dad says I rattle on."

"I don't mind," I said. I pushed half my sandwich toward her. "Would you like some?"

"Mmmm, I'll take a bite," she said, "even though you didn't like my beef stew."

"I just wasn't hungry for it," I said quickly.

She took a big bite of the Swiss cheese sandwich. "This is *won*-derful! Don't mind me, I'm just teasing about the beef stew. I tease all the time."

She pushed the rest of the sandwich back to me. "No, you can eat it," I said. I pushed it back to her.

"Thank you, Joyce," she said. "That's very sweet of you."

I saw Sharon Mason and Linda Justice staring at us from across the room. I bet they were surprised to see me sitting with someone so nice as Lacey!

"I like your name," I said. "I think it's pretty."

She leaned toward me, smiling. The way her front teeth stuck out made her look even nicer and prettier. "Do you really think my name is pretty, Joyce? Do you really think so? Lots of people think it's funny. When I say my name is Lacey, they laugh."

"No, I think it's really pretty. Joyce is just plain, but I like it because it's my mother's name, too."

"It is? You're Joyce Junior, then! I'll call you JJ," Lacey said. "Is that all right with you, JJ?"

"Yes," I said. I never had a special nickname before.

Lacey was in Miss Fontaine's class. Why couldn't she be in my room, instead of people like RB Byrd and Sharon Mason? "I wish you were in my class," I said.

"I wish I was in your class, too," Lacey said.

We talked all through lunch period. It went so fast I was really surprised. Usually I ate my lunch very slowly, and still there was always extra time. I folded my wax paper and my lunch bag. Lacey had a lunch box. "Nobody uses lunch boxes here, do they?" she said, looking around.

"You can get some lunch bags tomorrow," I said, "and start using them on Monday. Want to know something? I have a contest with myself to see how many times I can use the same lunch bag."

"Oh, neat, JJ," she said.

"My record is fifteen times."

Lacey laughed. "Fifteen times! I'm going to do that," she said. "We'll have a contest with each other." She looked at the clock. "Oh!" she said. "The bell's going to ring in ten minutes. Oh! I wish it would never ring."

"That's just what I was thinking," I said.

"I know," she said. "I could tell. Sometimes I can really tell what people are thinking just by looking at their faces!"

"What am I thinking now?" I said.

Lacey leaned toward me until our noses almost touched. "You—are—thinking—that—you—like—me—a—*lot*." She pressed her nose against mine until my eyes crossed looking at her. "Owls' eyes!" she said. She was so much fun! I wished lunch period would never end.

"Want to come to my house after school?" she said.

"I can't."

"Oh! Why not?"

"I have to help my Old Dad." I almost told her where I lived. Then I didn't. "I have to help him with his work." She looked sad, so I said, "We'll eat lunch together next week, on Monday."

"What about Tuesday?" she said.

"Tuesday, too," I said.

Sharon Mason walked by our table and gave us a very high-class look. I hoped Lacey didn't notice.

Lacey leaned toward me. "Want to know a secret? Swear to never tell?" I nodded. "I suck my thumb at night," she whispered. She put her hand over her heart. "Oh! I shouldn't have told you. Now you'll hate me."

"No, I won't," I said. I would never hate her.

"Now you have to tell me a secret," she said.

First, I told her about my mother's car accident. "But that's not the real secret," I said, and I told her how I thought maybe my mother had amnesia and would come back to me and Old Dad some day. I made her promise not to tell anyone. She swore and said we were friends. I felt so happy.

The rest of that day was almost all wonderful, too. When I got home from school Old Dad said we would close the dump early and drive to town to sell our paper, rags, and metal. That was one of my favorite things to do.

We loaded Lotsa Trouble, our pickup truck, LT for short. LT was faded red and rattled like a tin can full of stones. We drove into the city to Olsen and Farson, the junk dealers. It was an enormous place surrounded with a wooden fence. Inside were some low buildings and offices, and then everything else was bales of rags and paper, and huge heaps of metal. And everywhere you looked were old bashed-up cars waiting for the machine that pressed them flat. Old Dad liked Olsen and Farson for two reasons. One was that we made money from them. And two was that they saved stuff that was no good to people anymore, just like we did at the dump.

We drove through the gate and onto a big platform with a clock over it. Only it wasn't a clock, and it wasn't a platform. It was a huge scale.

A woman in jeans and a blue work cap wrote down what we weighed loaded up. "Okay. Unload the paper and rags," she said. We threw that stuff off and she weighed us again. Then Old Dad drove the truck across the lot, and we dumped the metal. I worked on the truck, pushing stuff to the back so Old Dad could lift it off. Then onto the scale one more time.

"Got it," the woman in the blue cap said. "Pay you in the office." In the office she opened the cash register and gave Old Dad a clean crispy five-dollar bill, a clean crispy ten-dollar bill, and fifty-five cents.

Over fifteen dollars! I poked Old Dad. That was really good. Then I saw the woman staring at Old Dad. I knew that look! She was bug-eyed, as if she never saw anybody like him before. As if, now, for the first time, she was taking a long good look at him, and couldn't believe what she saw. I stared back at her, but she didn't even notice.

Old Dad took out his wallet. He tucked in the money, then closed the wallet. He took out his little swan's-head purse and put in the change. The woman kept on staring at him. Old Dad put his wallet and purse in his back pocket. Then he fixed the brim of his work cap. It seemed as if everything was happening very slowly. It was terrible. It was like a dream where you can't make anything change, no matter how much you want to. My heart was beating slow and hard. I wanted to make Old Dad hurry, and I couldn't. I wanted to make her stop staring, and I couldn't. And with every second that passed, I saw Old Dad the way she was seeing him.

I saw that his eyes were little and close-set. I saw that his mouth was thin and flat, and that his arms were long, and his shoulders sloping. I saw that woman thinking, *He looks like an ape.* But the worst part of all was that I was thinking the same thing.

"Let's *go*," I said. We walked out. I started to get in the truck, then I turned and ran back into the office. The woman was picking up the phone. I wanted to say something terrible to her. Something to hurt her!

"Yes?" she said. She smiled at me. "Did you forget something?"

I shook my head. I ran out.

In the truck I didn't say anything for a long time. When we were almost out of town, I said, "Old Dad, why do you work in the dump? Why don't you work someplace else, like—" I stopped.

Old Dad finished the words for me. "—Like other men?"

"No, I didn't mean—"

"Yeah, you did! I ain't like other men."

My throat went tight and hot. I felt the way I did when the woman stared at him. Mad at her, and sad and mad at myself. I wanted to shout, *Yes, you are like other men. You're better than any of them.*

"I work in their dump," he said, "and I take their garbage. I take all their junk. I bury it, and I sort it, and I save it, and I give some of it back to 'em if it can be used again. I show them they don't have to throw away all that stuff." He sounded proud. "I show them that garbage has got its good sides. It don't have to be all waste, and throwing away, and stinking, and mucking up the earth. You see?" he said to me.

I nodded. "I see."

"Somebody has got to do it."

"They need you," I said.

"They sure do," he said. He poked me. "Besides—" He stopped for a red light. He gave me a sly look and let his lips slide over each other. "I'm the Ape!" He hunched his head and scratched under his arms, making hollow ape sounds. "Hoot . . . hooot . . . hoooooot. . . ."

We both laughed so hard we didn't see the light turn green. The car behind us honked and honked. And that made us laugh twice as hard.

When we got home the sun was going down and the sky was pink and green. Our house looked like it was waiting for us. It was small and plain. Old Dad had built it a long time ago, before I came to live with him. It was all unpainted wood which the weather had turned silvery.

Inside it was really snug because right in the middle of our downstairs room was a big black iron wood-burning stove. We had a plain wood table and two wooden chairs. People were always throwing away wooden chairs. We could have had a hundred if we wanted to, but we didn't like to have more than we needed. There were wooden shelves on the walls for our dishes and pots, and a big wooden box with a lid for our blankets and sheets. We had just what we needed, and no more.

In one corner of the room was Old Dad's bed. Old Dad liked wood better than almost anything, but his bed was brass. Every time I looked at it, I was surprised that anyone would ever throw it away. It had four tall brass posts, and it was beautiful.

After we ate supper, Old Dad went outside. I followed

him. The moon was out, big and round and yellow. I could see Face Pole by its light, leaning up against our house.

A long time go Face Pole was just a dead tree Old Dad hauled out of the woods for burning. He cut off all the branches and stacked them. He was all set to saw up the trunk. Then he saw a face in one of the knots. He started carving on it, and he's been carving ever since.

It started out to be just faces. That's why, when I was a little girl, I called it Face Pole. But now there were animals, too. Turtles, fish, deer, cats, and even a butterfly. Everywhere you looked, up and down, round and round, the pole was full of faces and animals. You thought you'd seen everything, and suddenly you saw something else.

In the moonlight I climbed the ladder. I started at the top of Face Pole and looked at all the faces and mouths and wings and feet and claws and ears of all the animals and birds and beasts. Some of the faces were huge and scary with big bursting eyes and twisting mouths. But I knew Face Pole was good. I looked at everything. When I came down from the ladder I had a strange dizzy feeling, as if I'd just come out of a dream.

I sat down on the bench next to Old Dad. I heard an owl, the one that whinnies like a horse. I heard the wind in the trees. I heard a mouse scooting by, and then the owl that sounds like a barking dog. I looked up at the moon. If I listened, and listened, and listened, could I hear the moon? If ever I heard the moon it would probably be the most beautiful sound in the world, something like hearing a bird sing, very far away, high and clear.

4

Crazy Fish

"I'm looking for bottles," a lady said, smiling at me. "Old bottles." She wore baby-blue pants and a baby-blue blouse. She had huge diamond rings on both hands.

"We have some bottles right here." I showed her the big wooden packing box where I put all the unbroken bottles.

"Oh, this is wonderful!" She took out one bottle at a time with the tips of her fingers. She looked at each bottle, then set it aside on the ground. After she'd taken out about twenty bottles, she found one she liked.

It was a tall bottle with a long narrow neck. It was filthy, but the lady said, "Oh, this is wonderful!"

She bent over headfirst into the packing case. The bottles clinked and clanked. When she straightened up, her hair was messed up and her baby-blue blouse was smudged. There were bottles all over the ground. "Well, I guess there's no more this time," she said.

I started putting the bottles back into the packing case. "Here you are, dear," the lady said. She gave me a dollar. I put it in my pocket. "Well, where are your manners?" she said. "Aren't you going to say thank you?"

My face got hot. "Thank you."

"You're *quite* welcome," she said, getting into her car. It was a blue Cadillac that matched her pants and blouse.

Old Dad and I ate our lunch on the bench outside the work shack. I gave him the dollar. He gave it back to me. "Yours." He showed me a pair of boots he'd salvaged. "See if they fit, Joyce."

I tried them on. They had thick soles with no cracks in them. The uppers were real leather and just worn a little bit. "I like them," I said.

"They're for you," Old Dad said, taking a bite of cold boiled potato.

I remembered the blue lady. "Thank you, Old Dad!"

All weekend I had good feelings thinking about Lacey Laurence, and Monday when we would eat lunch together again. But on Monday Lacey wasn't in the cafeteria at lunchtime. Tuesday morning I thought I would go to Lacey's room and ask her teacher where she was. But first I had to go to my own room for roll call.

As soon as I walked in I knew something was happening. Kids were looking at me and . . . waiting. I saw the waiting smiles on their faces. I sat down. Then I saw the blackboard. Someone had drawn a stick figure covered with garbage. It was even coming out of the ears. Next to it was another stick-figure drawing holding its nose with one hand, its other hand on his throat, gagging from the terrible smell.

I didn't say anything. I didn't move. I couldn't. I just sat at my desk with my neck quivering. The door opened. Mr. LaSorta walked in. He dropped his briefcase on the desk. " 'Morning, everybody," he said.

"Oh, Mr. LaSorta," Linda Justice said in a loud voice, "look at the awful pictures on the board. Want me to erase them?"

Linda had red hair and was Sharon's best friend. I
looked over at Sharon. She was reading her geography
book. Now I knew she and Linda drew those pictures.

Mr. LaSorta glanced around. "Who has the terrific
sense of humor?" He shook his head and erased the pictures. "Whoever is the secret artist, I want you to know I
just showered this morning. So you can stop holding your
nose." He sat down smoothing both sides of his long
droopy mustache.

"Not you, man!" somebody called from the back of the
room.

"I can't imagine it's anyone else in this room." He
looked all around, as if he was saying, *Anybody want to dis-
agree with me?* Nobody did. He started taking roll call. By
that time I'd forgotten all about going to Lacey's room.

Later, I was sorry. She wasn't in the cafeteria again. I
sat at a table in the corner and ate my sandwich slowly so
I wouldn't have time left over. But I still did, so I thought
about my mother. *One day, in the place where she's living and
doesn't know who she is, she was eating a cheese sandwich and
choked and fell over unconscious and bumped her head. When she
came to, the bump had made her remember everything. She remembered she had a daughter, Joyce, and came for me. But Old
Dad said, "I can't let my Joyce go." So my mother said, "I understand. In that case, we'll all live together." She moved in with us.
She slept upstairs in my attic room with me. Lacey came to meet
her. "You're so lucky!" Lacey said. "Your mother is beautiful.
And she has perfect manners!"*

The bell rang. I folded my wax paper and lunch bag
carefully. With every fold I made a wish. *Lacey, Lacey,
come back to school tomorrow.*

Lacey wasn't in school Wednesday, or Thursday either.
That was the bad part of those days. The good part was
that no one made up poems or put pictures on the black-

board. But Thursday afternoon when I was getting my stuff from my locker, RB Byrd and Michael Stacey walked past me.

"I smell something," Michael Stacey said in his silly voice. He has big teeth and freckles all over his cheeks.

"Oh, man, it stinks around here," RB said. He and Michael sniffed the air like a couple of dogs.

I banged my locker shut. *If they say one more thing, I'll punch them out.* I was all ready to do it. But just then, Mrs. Fish, the new custodian, came down the hall, pushing a big metal trash can on wheels. RB poked Michael. Michael poked RB.

"Look who's coming," RB said.

"Crazy Fish," Michael said. He and RB laughed like maniacs.

Last year Charlie was our custodian. Now we had Mrs. Fish. She was wearing blue-and-white striped railroad overalls, and a yellow ribbon bow in her hair. She was tall and fat. She was singing to herself, and as she pushed the trash can down the hall, kids followed her, putting their fingers in their ears and making the crazy sign at their foreheads.

Someone called, "Oh, hoo ha! There's Crazy Fish!"

The hall was full of kids. All the kids started saying it. "Oh, hoo ha! There's Crazy Fish!"

Kids ran up and down the hall. "Pass it along. Oh, hoo ha! There's Crazy Fish!"

Mrs. Fish heard them. I know she did. But she just smiled and picked up a wad of paper from the floor. She tossed the paper into her can with a flip of her wrist. Then, just as if it was part of her cleaning job, she twirled around. She was dancing for the kids! One hand was raised so prettily, and the other hand was on her waist.

She spun around. Her fat stomach and her fat breasts and her fat butt jiggled and bounced. Everyone was laughing and calling. Some girls clapped their hands in time to her dancing.

I stood there, staring at her. My face was burning. I hated her. I hated Mrs. Fish. I didn't even know her, and I hated her! She was making a fool of herself. My fists clenched. "Stop it," I said. "Stop it. Stop it!"

❦ 5 ❧

Popeye the Sailor Man

"Some friend you are," Lacey said. She stared at me hard. I didn't understand. I took a bite of sandwich. "Well, aren't you going to say *anything*?" Lacey tossed her long brown hair over her shoulder.

"Where were you?" I said. It was Friday and we were in the lunchroom. I was so glad to see Lacey at last, and now she was mad at me, and I didn't know why.

"I was sick!" Lacey said. "I was sick with a cold. What did you *think*?"

I chewed and chewed. It was hard to swallow. "That's what I thought," I said at last. "I thought you were sick."

"Then how come you didn't call me up?"

"Call you up?"

"Telephone," she said. "New invention. You talk into it, and the person at the other end hears you and talks back. *Hello, Lacey, this is Joyce. Hello, Joyce, this is Lacey.*" She wasn't smiling.

I kept chewing the same soggy bite of sandwich. I spit it into my hand and put it on my wax paper.

"Yuuuck!" Lacey said. "How disgusting! Cover it up!"

My face got hot. I folded the wax paper over the chewed-up bite. Sometimes Old Dad spit out food if it was too tough. But I shouldn't have.

"Well?" Lacey said.

"We don't have a phone."

"You don't have a phone?"

I shook my head.

"How come?"

"I don't know. We just don't."

"Are you telling me the truth, Joyce Adams?"

"Yes." My hands and face were hot and sweaty. "I wouldn't lie to you."

"Swear to God," Lacey said.

"Swear to God!" I said.

"Cross your heart and hope to die!"

"Cross my heart and hope to die," I said.

"Swear on your mother's grave."

I gasped and covered my mouth. "Don't say that!"

"I'm sorry," Lacey said. "I forgot. I didn't mean to hurt your feelings, Joyce."

"That's all right," I said. "I didn't want to hurt yours either."

Lacey smiled at me. "Now we each have something to be mad at the other one for, so we're even. Here, put up your hand against mine." We put up our hands together. "Even Steven Leaven Kleaven, May you and I be friends forever! Now you say E-S-L-K-F-F."

"E-S-L-K-F-F," I said.

Lacey dropped her hand. "We're made up. I'm glad you don't have a phone, Joyce. I thought you didn't care."

"I care," I said. "I care a lot. You're my best friend."

"Before, where I came from in Youngstown," Lacey

said, "I had three best friends. Marcia, Mary, and Laura. Everyone called us the L and M's." She smiled. Her eyes were the same red brown as oak leaves in the fall. "Who was your best friend before me?"

"No one," I said.

"*No one.* How could you have no best friend?"

"Guess what?" I said quickly. "Where we live the deer come to be fed when the weather gets cold. They come right to our door and we feed them."

"Oh, I have to see that, Joyce! Promise I can come? I'll stay over your house. Okay?"

No one ever stayed over with me. I thought about Lacey and me up in my attic room. I'd show her my bottles. We'd tell each other all our wishes and dreams. We'd call down to Old Dad, *Good night!* But that was a long way off. "You can come," I said, "if we're still best friends."

"If?" Lacey said, putting her hand on her heart. "If! Joyce! Are you going to leave me and be best friends with someone else? Are you still mad at me for saying that about your mother's grave?"

"No," I said. "You're my best friend."

"I'm not fickle," Lacey said. "We'll always be best friends."

The bell rang. We promised to meet on Monday. I felt so happy. *Monday I'll tell Lacey where I live and how Old Dad runs the dump. She'll say, "A dump! Joyce! I've got to see it. Promise I can come see it. Promise I can ride on the baby dozer, too!"*

I was whistling when I walked into my classroom. I smelled something queer, but I didn't pay any attention. But when I opened my desk to get out my notebook, I saw where the smell was coming from. My desk was full of slimy, smelly garbage.

I wanted to slam down the desk, but I didn't. I felt

frozen. Kids were whispering. Mr. LaSorta said, "Let's settle down, folks."

If he tells me to clean it up, I won't do it.

"Mr. LaSorta," I said at last.

"Joyce?"

Everyone was looking at me. I made myself stand up straight. "I won't sit at this desk!"

Mr. LaSorta came down the aisle and looked in my desk. He sighed. He looked all around the room. He ran his finger down one side of his mustache, then down the other side.

"Okay." He sighed again. "Will you get the custodian please, Joyce? Tell her to bring a bucket with her."

When he said *bucket* the whole class fell apart laughing, as if *bucket* was the funniest word they'd ever heard.

"Okay! Okay! Settle down!" Mr. LaSorta yelled.

I went out of the room. I was halfway down the hall when I remembered I didn't have a pass. If the principal saw me he'd ask for my pass. I ran back to our room and opened the door.

". . . because she has a slightly different situation than most of you," Mr. LaSorta was saying, "is no reason to—" Then he saw me and he stopped talking. Everyone looked at me. He was talking about me! Trying to make the kids feel sorry for me. I backed out. I pounded down the hall. Let the principal catch me. I wished he would. I ran down the steps, down to the basement to the custodian's room.

I could hear Mrs. Fish talking inside. "Oh, my aching feet! These sneakers cost me eight dollars, and my feet hurt in them. William, I can remember when sneakers cost ninety-nine cents. Yes, I can! Don't look at me like that. Oh, a long time ago, when I was a girl and Mama was living."

I waited. There was somebody in there with her. I

didn't want to knock on the door. Maybe she would come out.

"William, I think I'll go down to the variety store tonight after work and buy one of those cute pink baby tubs to soak my feet. Warm salt water, that's the best thing for aching feet. Mama always said so. She was also a bit on the heavy side, and her feet hurt her, too. Now, don't say I ought to go on a diet—" Mrs. Fish giggled. Her voice was high like a little girl's. "I like Mrs. Fish just the way she is," she said.

It didn't sound as if she was ever going to stop talking. And I couldn't stand there forever. I knocked. In a moment the door opened. I had to look up to see her. She was wearing the striped railroad overalls again over a white sweat shirt. She had red-and-white striped bows in her hair, one on each side.

"Who're you?" she said.

"Joyce Adams. Mr. LaSorta wants you to go to his room with a bucket." I looked around. There was nobody in the room. Only an orange-and-white cat sitting on a table.

"What has to be cleaned up?" Mrs. Fish said. There was a string tied around her middle, and a bunch of keys hanging from the string. Up close like this, I could see short, stiff black whiskers on her chin.

"A desk needs cleaning," I said.

"What's wrong with the desk?"

"There's stuff in it." I turned to go. She held me. Her hand was strong.

"Stuff, stuff, what sort of stuff?"

"Garbage," I said.

"Garbage in a desk? Why?"

"Because."

"Because why?" She didn't let go of my arm.

"Me," I said. I hated her. I hated her black whiskers. I hated her fat bosoms which were right in front of my face. I hated her squeaky voice, and the ribbons in her hair.

"Me," she said. "Me. What do you mean, me? What kind of me are you to have garbage in your desk?"

She thought I put the garbage in my own desk! I hated her more for being so stupid! "They put it in!" I was shivering. "They put garbage in my desk! *They* did it! I didn't put it there." My voice cracked. I was crying. I didn't want to cry. "Let me *go*."

But Mrs. Fish wasn't holding my arm so hard anymore. She was stroking it and patting my back. I could smell her skin smell, like lemons and soap. "Why, you poor baby," she said. "There, there, little one, go on, cry, cry all you want." Then somehow she had both arms around me and I was leaning against her fat bosoms and I didn't hate her anymore.

She made me sit down. She put the cat in my lap. "This is William," she said.

"I know," I said.

"Oh, you've met. How nice." She handed me a cup of tea. "Drink, little one, it will make you feel better." The cat was heavy and warm in my lap. He sniffed my arm, then leaned his chin on it.

Mrs. Fish sat down across from me. "Garbage in her desk." She whistled through her front teeth, snorted, and shook her head. "Drink the tea. Listen to Mrs. Fish, she knows what's best for feeling bad."

I sipped the tea. It was hot and sweet, and I could feel it going down into my belly. "It's good," I said.

Her room was small with just one high window. The window had bars on it. On a shelf were an electric hot

plate, a teapot with daisies painted on it, a glass jar stuffed
with tea bags, a red Roy Rogers lunch box, and a bunch of
colored cups and plates. There were pictures all over the
room, some of them taped to the walls, some in frames
hanging on nails. All the pictures were of animals. Under
the window was a picture of a white mother cat and three
little black baby kittens. Below that was a picture of two
horses racing through tall grass, and next to that was another picture of a spaniel rolling on his back.

"I like your pictures," I said.

"Aren't they beautiful?" Mrs. Fish said. "But not as
beautiful as my William and Greta. Greta's my dog," she
explained. "She stays home. But William likes to come to
school with me, and I let him because he's so well be-
haved. How do you feel now?"

"Okay," I said.

Mrs. Fish winked. "A hot drink in time of trouble,
that's what Mama always said. And it never fails, little
one."

"My name is Joyce."

"Think I forgot that?" She whistled through her teeth.
"Mrs. Fish isn't dumb, little one." She took a mop, a
bucket, rags, a bag, and a bottle of detergent from a closet.
"I'm off to clean up the mess," she said. "You sit right
here for a while. You don't want to go back and show
them your red eyes, do you?"

I shook my head and petted William. "I'm sorry about
crying," I said.

"Tush on that," Mrs. Fish said. "A good cry is worth-
while. Now sit here and look around. Then pretty soon
you go back up there like nothing ever happened."

She was singing as she went to the door. "I yam Popeye
the Sailor Man, I live in a garbage can. . . ." She butted
open the door. "I yam what I yam. . . ."

The door closed behind her. I heard her singing as she went down the hall. "I yam Popeye the Sailor Man. . . ."

I sat there for a long time looking at the pictures of animals on the walls. William curled up and slept. It would be nice to be a cat. I wished the day was over.

◆ 6 ◆

Garbage Pie

A man drove into the dump in a green pickup truck. "Got some stuff to dump, old-timer," he said to Old Dad. "Roofing."

Old Dad pointed him to the fill pit. That's where we throw plastic, tar, oil, all the things that won't break down in the earth, and can't be used again. Old Dad thought the man had asphalt roofing. But it was cedar shingles. Good wood!

"Hey, you! Back up," Old Dad yelled. His hoarse growly voice always made him sound as if he was really mad.

The man's head jerked up. "What's the matter, old-timer?" He leaned out the window of his truck.

"Over there! Over there!" Old Dad growled, pointing to the wood pile. "Stack it up, Joyce."

As fast as the man threw off the shingles I stacked them by the road to our house. I could almost smell that cedar burning in our stove. I love a cedar fire, and a pine fire. Both smell so good that, even if you're sitting right in front of the stove, if you close your eyes and sniff you can imagine you're really out in the woods.

The man kicked off the last few shingles, then threw down a bulging green plastic bag. Out spilled a bunch of yellow squashes.

"Hey!" Old Dad pointed to the squashes. "That's good food."

The man shrugged. "We got too much out of the garden."

"That'll keep. Squash winters."

"The wife don't like squash. I should never have planted it." He drove away.

I put the squashes near the wood. There were eight of them, all as big as bowling pins. We hadn't grown squash in our garden, so I was really happy to get them. All morning as I worked I thought about squash pie and baked squash and squash cooked with tomatoes and good-smelling herbs like basil and marjoram. But I didn't get to cook them that night. I was too tired when we went back to the house.

Sunday morning the sun was shining, bouncing bits of gold and blue and green against the wall. I lay in bed, stretching and wriggling my toes. The sun coming through my colored glass was so pretty! I loved my room. It's all wood with slanting wooden walls. When Old Dad built his house he made one big room for himself. Then I came to live with him, and he fixed up the attic for me. I have a wooden bed, shelves around the walls, and an oak bureau with four drawers.

When I went downstairs I told Old Dad, "I'm going to make squash pie today." He nodded. "Do you like squash pie?"

"That's okay," he said.

"I can make something else."

"Okay."

"Squash pie or squash casserole?"

"Either one," he said.

"Choose, Old Dad," I ordered. "Choose one!"

"Squash pie's okay," he said.

"You choose that?"

"Okay."

"You sure?"

He nodded.

"Say it, Old Dad. Say 'I choose squash pie!' "

"Hey, you!" he growled just the way he did to the man in the green truck. "Eat your breakfast."

"Say you choose squash pie first," I said. "It's no fun cooking if you don't *want* it."

Old Dad scowled and pulled at his lip. "Okay, okay! Squash pie."

"I'm glad you said that," I said, going to the refrigerator for milk, "because I love squash pie."

"Crazy girl!" Old Dad was laughing in that special way he has, without any sound.

We had a shelf of cookbooks that people threw away. *Uncle John's Bread Book. The Winter Garden Cookbook. Chinese Cooking. The Bride's Basic Cookbook. Simple Spanish Meals.* Sometimes I picked one of our cookbooks, closed my eyes, and opened it anywhere. Whatever page it opened to, I had to cook something from that page. Mostly I cooked on Sundays, because the rest of the week I was too tired or too busy. And the same was true of Old Dad. If he got in the mood on Sunday, he'd make chili, or fish soup.

While I was baking the squash pie, Old Dad worked outside on Face Pole. That was his favorite thing to do on Sundays. When the weather got too cold to work outside, he'd bring Face Pole into the house and lay it down on the floor beneath the front windows. It was sixteen feet long, exactly as long as our house one way.

When the squash pies were done, Old Dad ate three pieces steaming hot. But we still had plenty left over. In the morning I wrapped a big piece in wax paper for Lacey. It was perfect when I wrapped it, but when I took it out at lunchtime it was squishy and sticking to the paper.

"That's not the way it's supposed to be," I said.

"Why didn't you put it in a plastic pie dish?" Lacey said.

"We don't have any plastic in our house."

"You don't? Mmm, this is yummy! How about waste-baskets?"

I shook my head. "Eat all you want," I said. "I have more at home."

"I bet you have a plastic glass in your house," Lacey said, spooning up another bite of pie. "At *least* one plastic glass."

"Not a one," I said. "Nothing plastic."

"Why not?" Lacey said, finishing the pie.

"Because plastic isn't real. Old Dad only likes real things."

Lacey tossed her long brown hair over her shoulder. She had beautiful hair. I thought she was the most beautiful girl in the entire school.

"What do you mean, it's not real," she said. "That's the dumbest thing I ever heard."

"Not real like wood," I said. "Wood grows, and when it dies it rots into the ground. Did you ever see a plastic tree?"

"Sure," Lacey said, "they grow in the plastic woods."

Her eyes were shining. "What does Old Dad like, any-way?"

"Mostly stuff made out of wood and leather and brass and—"

"*Brass* trees?" Lacey said. We couldn't stop laughing. "Oh, we're nuts," Lacey said, as she cleaned the last little drop of squash pie off the wax paper.

Tuesday we sat together again, and every time one of us said, "Brass trees," we laughed so hard we had to hold our stomachs. But then, on Wednesday, no Lacey. I waited for her. I didn't open my lunch bag. I watched the clock. I thought, *She's sick. I'll go to the office and ask Miss Poushter to use the phone. I'll call her.*

But I had a strange feeling in my throat. When I was getting off the bus that morning, didn't I see Lacey going into school? Just as I was thinking that, Lacey walked into the lunchroom. I started to wave to her. Then I saw that she was with Sharon Mason and Linda Justice.

I watched the three of them cross the room and sit down. Linda combed her hair. Sharon whispered to Lacey. Their heads were touching, brown and brown.

It took me a long time to eat my sandwich. I didn't feel at all hungry. When I was finished I looked around. Lacey, Sharon, and Linda were gone. Maybe I made it all up! Maybe it was a dream. I had the same dizzy feeling I sometimes got when I looked too close at the animal faces on Face Pole.

At the end of the day I went to Lacey's room. Most of the kids were leaving, but she was talking to Miss Fontaine. I hung around, waiting for her. *What if it was a dream? I'll tell her—I thought I saw you with Linda and Sharon! And she'll say, "You nut, Joyce! Why would I want to go around with those snobs?"*

It was crowded in the halls. Someone bumped hard against me. "Watch it," I said, turning. It was RB Byrd.

RB opened his eyes wide. "Did I bump into you? Oh, pardon me, your Royal Highness."

Michael Stacey was right behind him. Quick, he bumped into me. "Oh, pardon me! Your Royal Royal Highness," he said.

I clenched my fists. "Screwballs! Jerks!" Then Lacey came out of her room and I forgot about them. We looked at each other. Lacey didn't say anything. And neither did I. Then, finally, I said, "Hi."

"Oh . . . hi." She tucked her hair behind her ears with one finger, first the left side, then the right side.

"Are we going to eat together tomorrow?" I said.

"What?" she said.

"I'm not talking Chinese!"

"What?" she said again.

I wanted to say, *Brass trees!* Then we'd laugh and everything would be the way it was. "Lacey," I said, "I thought we were going to eat together every day." I could feel my face getting red.

But Lacey's face was just smooth and pretty, soft and cool, like cream. "Why didn't you tell me you lived in a dump?" she said in a cool, creamy voice.

"I don't live in a dump."

"Oh, yes, you do. I know you do. Don't lie to me." Her voice got even softer. "You live in a garbage dump."

The softer her voice got, the louder mine got. "I thought we were best friends!"

"Best friends tell the truth," Lacey said.

"I was going to tell you!"

"You lie," Lacey said. "You live in a garbage dump, and you didn't tell me."

There was a choked-up feeling in my throat. I thought maybe I was close to crying, so I made mean eyes and said, "There's something else I didn't tell you. Yesterday . . . you ate garbage pie." Lacey gasped. "That wasn't no squash pie," I said. "That was garbage pie. Made out of *nice, fresh* garbage!"

"I'm going to throw up!" Lacey held her stomach. "Don't you ever talk to me again!"

I thought of all the times Old Dad had told me, *We don't need anybody but us, Joyce. The rest of them jerks can go jump in a lake.* "I'll talk to you if I want to," I said. "But I won't want to."

"Good," Lacey said. "That suits me."

"Go jump in a lake," I said, and I walked away. The halls were empty. Most of the kids were gone. Mrs. Fish was mopping near the gym. She squinted at me. "Who's that?"

Why didn't she remember me? "It's Joyce," I said. The choked feeling in my throat was bad.

She swept the mop in a big swooshy circle on the floor. She swished the water round and round, and mopped up to me. "Oh, *Joyce.* Now I see you."

"You saw me before."

"Why, dear one, no, I'm a trifle nearsighted. All I saw was a little blob." She winked at me. "The doctor wants me to wear glasses, but I told him, 'Glasses are for old ladies, doctor dear!' " She pushed the mop around, dancing with it. "You're going home now? Toodle-oo, Joyce."

It was drizzling when I left school. I'd missed the bus. Five miles to our house. That was okay. I liked walking in the rain. Besides, now I didn't have to see Sharon or Linda, or any of them.

All the way home I thought of things I could have said

to Lacey. And more things I could have said to RB Byrd and stupid Michael Stacey. It was always like this. I never thought of any of it until afterward. Then it was too late.

Maybe I should write them all letters.

Dear Lacey, You're a traitor. Why did you promise to be my best friend, if you didn't mean it? Talk about lies! That's the biggest lie I ever heard. For your information, the dump is extremely clean and well kept, and if you knew my Old Dad you would like him very much. You would even love him.

Dear RB Byrd, I hate your very guts.

Dear Sharon and Linda, You stink like old garbage.

Dear Mrs. Fish (since I was writing letters, I would write her, too), *I'm glad you're nearsighted and didn't forget me. But you should wear glasses. They aren't so terrible. I'm just lucky I have 20-20 vision. I bet you would even look pretty in glasses!*

Making up letters helped the time pass. Pretty soon I was home. I put on potatoes to boil for supper. We'd eat them with lots of butter. I picked tomatoes from our garden and peeled onions and garlic for Old Dad.

When Old Dad came in from the dump he was muttering to himself, and he forgot to change before he sat down at the table. "Change your shirt, Old Dad."

"Huh?"

"Your shirt!"

He stomped off to change. When he came back I asked him what happened. He shook his head and speared a potato. "Jerks!"

"Somebody made you mad," I said.

"Big six-foot slob," Old Dad said. "Had his little kid with him. Boy doesn't come up to his daddy's knee." He speared another potato, then shook his fork at me. "Kid got himself dirty, and his father walloped him. Knocked him down. I told him," Old Dad said. "I told him, 'I don't allow no hitting no little kids here!' "

"What'd he say?"

Old Dad snorted. "He says, 'Since when do apes tell men how to behave?' So I says, 'Since right now! Get out of my dump and don't come back.' "

I jumped up and hugged Old Dad. "You said that?"

"Hey, sit down and eat. You're slobbering all over me."

That night I went upstairs to bed early. The rain had stopped, and there was a moon out. It was shining in my window. I cuddled Mama Big Joyce Doll and watched the clouds go over the moon.

Downstairs I heard Old Dad getting ready for bed. I heard him shut the windows and turn off the lights.

I thought of all the things that had happened that day. Bad things and good things. Lacey and Mrs. Fish. That man calling Old Dad an ape. Old Dad telling him never to come to the dump again! Wish I could have seen his face. Guess he won't call anybody an ape so fast, next time.

The moonlight was soft on my face. I closed my eyes and began to write another letter in my head.

Dear Mother, Wherever you are, I love you. Tonight the moon is bright. My eyes are closed. Isn't it funny you can't feel moonshine on your face the way you feel sunshine?

Then I fell asleep.

❦ 7 ❧

The Dump Queen

Steven, the little boy with the briefcase, got on the school bus. Behind him was Sharon Mason, then me. "Right here, Sharon," Linda Justice called, patting the seat next to her.

I walked past them. "Here comes her Royal Highness," RB Byrd sang out. "Here comes her Royal Highness, the Queen of the Latrine!"

I sat down next to Lila Martin Parton. That's her real name. "Hi, Marty," I said.

"Hi." She has long long skinny legs, and long long skinny arms. She twisted her legs to make room for me.

"Marty!" Linda Justice called, "Don't you even care if you get cooties?"

"Cooties!" Marty jumped up, stepped on my feet, and sat down across the aisle. I slid over next to the window.

"The Queen has cooties," someone said. "Pass it on."

The bus stopped for more kids. A first-grade kid sat down next to me. "Don't sit there!" about six people yelled. "That's the Cootie Queen."

Then Sharon Mason said, "No, that's the *Dump* Queen. Joyce is the Dump Queen!"

And everybody started saying it. "Joyce is the Dump Queen."

I looked out the window. The fields were all purple and yellow with goldenrod and asters. Later, I'd pick a bunch when I got home and put them in a jar on the table. Or maybe I'd take them upstairs to my room. Then I could see the flowers in the morning while I was getting dressed. That would be nice.

That morning, first thing, we had music. In the music room we took our places on the platform. "Everybody! Ready?" Mrs. Oglethorpe said. She had a big head of curly hair. "Let's all limber up the throats with a scale. Do-oooooo," she sang and lifted her hands.

"Do-ooooo," we sang.

Music was one of my favorite classes. Mrs. Oglethorpe let us sing as loud as we wanted. After the scales we sang, "Do, a deer, a female deer, re, a drop of golden sun. . . ." That song gave me shivers. Usually, no matter what we were singing, I didn't think about *anything* else. But that morning in music, and all morning long, I heard the whispering around me. *Bzzz . . . bzzz . . . bzzzz . . .* Like insects.

"*Bzzzz . . .* the Dump Queen . . . pass it on . . . *bzzzz . . .* she stinks. . . . Don't let her touch you . . . you'll get cooties. . . . *Bzzzz . . .* the Dump Queen . . ."

At lunchtime I went outside on the playground and sat down on a rock. I was afraid to go in the cafeteria. The sun was shining, and the wind was blowing, and the trees across the street were red and yellow. Some of the yellow leaves were falling in the wind.

Kids were playing around, but nobody paid any attention to me. After a while I felt better. I folded my wax paper and started telling myself a story. *In Pennsylvania there's a very lovely woman who works in a restaurant . . . the best waitress they ever had. . . . She has yellow hair, and walks with her head so high and smells so good people call her The Queen. No one knows where The Queen came from. . . . She lives all alone . . . she's always very lovely . . . speaks in a soft voice and makes people feel good. . . . She really—*

"Dinga dinga dunga dunga!" A long snaky line of kids with their arms around each other's waists was heading straight for me. "Out of the way," they sang, "out of the way, here comes the Queen of the Dump. Out of the way, out of the way, dinga dinga dunga dunga JUMP!" At the last moment they all jumped away from me.

Then they turned, snaking around, and came toward me again. More kids joined in. There must have been twenty-five or thirty kids, all holding each other's waists, singing and chanting. Kids from my class, and kids from other classes, kids I knew, and kids I didn't know.

"Out of the way . . . out of the way . . . here comes the Queen of the Dump. . . . Out of the way . . . out of the way . . . dinga . . . dinga . . . dunga . . . dunga . . . JUMP!"

I got up and walked toward the school. The kids scattered, screaming, "Don't let her touch you! Oh, phew!" I kept walking. Someone ran up to me. I couldn't tell who it was. The sun was too bright. My eyes were . . . almost *closing*.

"Dinga . . . dinga . . . dunga . . . dunga . . . JUMP!" The girl ran around me, yelling and making faces. She jumped in the air and poked her fingers at me. I grabbed for her.

"Oh, help," she screamed. "She touched me. Get it off

me!" She ran up to another girl and wiped her hand on her. "I pass it on to you!"

"It's a disease," the second girl cried. "A smelly disease. Save me!"

I went into the school. It was dark and cool inside. Lunch still wasn't over. I could hear the noise and voices from the cafeteria. I walked down the hall, down the stairs. I went all the way down to the basement. Near Mrs. Fish's room I slid along the wall and sat on the floor. I stretched out my legs.

The other day I thought the basement was spooky. But now I liked it. There was nobody around except me. I liked the darkness in the corners.

Mrs. Fish's door opened. She poked out her head. "Anybody there?"

"Me," I said.

She squinted over to where I was sitting. Her hair was like a big messy gray cloud, and in the cloud were two big black-and-orange butterflies.

"Joyce?"

"Yes."

"Well, come in!" I got up. Mrs. Fish stood at her door, holding it open with her arm. "Welcome! Welcome!"

In her room I sat down and William jumped right into my lap. "William welcomes you, too," Mrs. Fish said. She put her hands into her hair. The butterflies were *barrettes*. They were beautiful.

"Joyce . . . Joyce . . ." Mrs. Fish stroked her black whiskers. "What will it be, dear one? Tea and cookies? Chocolate chippers? Or graham crackers?"

I dragged my eyes away from the butterfly barrettes. Through the little window I saw feet running past on the playground. "Graham crackers?" I said. I felt very tired.

Mrs. Fish clapped her hands. "I was hoping you'd say that." She wore an orange sweater buttoned up over her overalls. The buttons were little silver cats.

A kettle was boiling on the hot plate. She put out cups and poured boiling water in them. She dropped a tea bag in each cup, letting the white string with the little red tag stick out. She took a yellow canister off the shelf, opened it, and took out a stack of graham crackers. She put the crackers on a flowered plate. Everything she had was pretty. Everything was decorated. There was a vase with red, orange, and yellow flowers on the table. I touched the flowers. "Are these artificial?"

"Certainly," Mrs. Fish said. She sat down. "Isn't this cozy?" She pushed the tea toward me. "Drink, dear one."

I took a sip and burned my tongue.

"No, no, you have to blow on it first." Mrs. Fish blew across the top of her cup, pursing her lips as if someone had pulled a string through them. "This way." She held her cup with her little finger raised. "Blow, then sip."

We sipped tea and ate graham crackers. The bell rang. Lots of feet ran past the window. Mrs. Fish climbed up on the chair and opened the window. Voices came floating in. Kids calling to each other. I put my face down in William's fur. I wished Mrs. Fish would come down off the chair and close the window.

"All those children," Mrs. Fish said. "I was watching them before. Running around. Singing."

I crumbled a graham cracker. My face was hot.

"You know what I say?" Mrs. Fish said. "I say, Tush on them all. Tush on them all, dear one! They are silly with me all the time, but they don't hurt me because I don't let them!"

The second bell rang. I got up. "I've got to go now." I

didn't want to go. My throat hurt. My eyes stung. It was so dumb! I didn't cry out on the playground.

"Now, now," Mrs. Fish said. She patted my back. "Just remember the kind people."

"What?"

"There were once many kind people," Mrs. Fish said in a singsong voice. "And there still are. You'll see, dear one, you'll see."

"Good-bye, Mrs. Fish." I went all the way to the stairs, then I remembered and ran back. "Mrs. Fish! Thank you."

"Oh, no, don't thank me." Her face colored. "I should thank you! When do I ever have such lovely company?"

I wished I could say, *Thank you, dear one!* Instead I said, "Tush on them all, Mrs. Fish." Then I went back to Mr. LaSorta's room.

❧ 8 ❧

Henery Fenery

Old Dad's paycheck was in the mailbox when I got off the school bus. I ran up the road waving the envelope. Old Dad was tinkering with a washing machine in one of the open sheds. "It's here! Your check is here, Old Dad!"

"Then get ready," he called.

When Old Dad's check came, we always went into town. We'd eat out, shop, and do our laundry. In the house I pulled the sheets off the bed and put them in the laundry bag. It was really a flour sack. It had a picture of a mill on it and over that HARTER'S MILL, BUCKWHEAT, RYE, STONE-GROUND WHOLE WHEAT. I shoved in all my laundry. Then I crawled under Old Dad's bed and pulled out the clothes he kicked under there every day.

I dragged the stuffed laundry bag outside and put it in the back of the pickup truck. I wiped the windows and the headlights and gave the fenders a quick going-over. It started to rain softly. I went back inside and changed my clothes and combed my hair. Then I got everything ready for Old Dad.

I took his green plaid shirt off the wall hook and laid it on his bed with the arms stretched out, all ready for him to put on. I put a fresh pair of socks next to the shirt. In the bathroom I made sure there was soap in the dish and a towel on the rack. Last, I poured a glass of orange juice and left it on the table.

I was hungry, but I didn't eat. It was better to be really hungry when we went into town. Then everything tasted doubly good. I stood at the window, waiting for Old Dad. I was impatient. I saw him coming down the path. "Run!" I said. He came rolling on, swinging his shoulders. He wouldn't run for anybody.

I swung open the door. "Come on! There's orange juice on the table. Your shirt's on the bed, and you—"

"Hey! Who you shouting at?"

"I'm not shouting. I'm just telling you something."

"Hold your horses."

I had to wait while he washed his hands and his arms and his neck and his ears. I thought he'd never get through washing! I walked around and around, waiting to hand him the towel. He dried himself slowly, rubbing his head and wiping his neck and face until they were boiling red.

"Old Dad! You're clean enough. You're going to rub your skin off."

He just grunted. He unbuttoned his shirt, then looked at me, frowning, and I turned my back. After he changed his shirt he got down on his knees and checked under his bed for laundry.

"I did that!" I said.

"Maybe you missed something."

"I didn't miss anything."

"Huh!" He stood up, triumphantly holding out a wool sock.

"Just one little sock," I said.

"Let's see what else you forgot."

"Old Dad!" I hopped around. "You won't find anything else," I said. "Nothing. Nothing!"

"You sure?"

"I'm sure, I'm sure," I cried. I knew he was teasing me but I couldn't tease back. "Let's go! Don't you want to go to town?"

He dusted off his knees and put on his plaid town jacket, then patted his pockets to make sure he had his wallet and keys. He drank the orange juice, took his paycheck, and finally we went outside and climbed into LT.

"Windows cleaned?" he said.

"I wiped them," I said. "Can't you tell! Headlights, too," I said fast, before he could ask.

He turned on the ignition. LT coughed, shook, rattled, then caught. I patted LT's cracked leather seat. "Never lets us down," Old Dad said.

In town we went to the laundromat first. It was almost empty. I measured soap into three machines while Old Dad got all the quarters together. When the machines were going, we crossed the road to a hamburger place.

"Two large burgers, two double fries, one vanilla milkshake, and one coffee," Old Dad said. People turned and stared. His voice was sort of loud. So what? Staring was worse.

We carried our tray to a table by a window. Right across from us was a family, one big kid, one little kid, and the parents. I watched them while we ate. The mother and the boy were sharing a cone of french fries. First she took one, then he took two, then she took one, then he took three. The father was feeding the little girl from his plate. In between bites of hamburger she looked around. She saw Old Dad, and he smiled at her. She ducked her head, then looked back, then ducked her head again.

Suddenly she twisted around and tried to reach across the aisle to Old Dad. "What's a name?" she said.

"Henry," Old Dad said.

"Henery?" she said.

Old Dad nodded. "Henery Fenery."

"Henery Fenery!" she repeated.

"Amy," her mother said, "turn around."

"Henery Fenery!" Amy said again.

Her father frowned. "Amy! You stop that." Amy's father looked at Old Dad.

"Henery Fenery!" Amy shouted, reaching out to Old Dad. He took her hand and shook it up and down. Didn't he see the look Amy's father was giving him?

"Old Dad," I whispered fiercely.

"You want some more fries?" he said.

"No! I'm done. Let's go." We swept our trays clean into the wastebasket.

"Henery Fenery, good-bye," Amy shouted. Old Dad waved to her. He was always nice to little children. Only, sometimes, their parents could be utterly DUMB.

In the laundromat we put our wash into the dryers. Then we drove to the Piggly Wiggly Market. "I'll cash the check," Old Dad said. "You start the shopping. Don't forget my Polish pickles." I got out of the car.

In the market I wheeled a basket slowly through the aisles. It was fun to look at all the things to buy. I put bread, milk, butter, and a pound of bacon in the basket. I was searching for the pickles when I almost ran into another cart.

"Whoa there," a familiar voice said.

"Mrs. Fish! What are you doing here?" She was pushing a cart piled high with food. I almost didn't recognize her because she was wearing a full green skirt with a pink blouse and a whole bunch of necklaces and chains.

"You look so pretty," I said.

"Why, Joyce! Thank you." She turned her cart around and we pushed through the aisles together. When we got into line Mrs. Fish pointed through the plate-glass window to the building across the street. "I live right over there, Joyce, on the second floor. It's a very convenient location."

It was almost my turn at the cash register. "I have to wait for Old Dad," I told Mrs. Fish. I got out of line and pushed my cart into a corner. I didn't have any money.

Mrs. Fish wheeled her full cart up to me. "Why don't you come up to my house and wait for your Old Dad?" she said. "You can watch out the window for him."

We carried her groceries across the street and up the stairs. The halls were dim and smelled like meat. A dog was barking in the front apartment. "Coming, Greta, coming, honey," Mrs. Fish called. As soon as Mrs. Fish opened the door, Greta started jumping up and down, really leaping into the air, shaking with happiness. She was a little gray poodle with tight curly hair and a wet black nose that looked just like the knob on a drawer.

"Hello, Greta. I'm Joyce." I let her smell my fingers. She sniffed both hands very carefully, then sat down and grinned at me, stretching her lips back and showing her teeth.

"She likes you," Mrs. Fish said. "I knew she would. Greta and I always like the same people. Oh, oh, here comes William. He can't stand Greta having all the attention."

William came toward me looking very dignified. He lifted each one of his white paws as if he was stepping in butter. He walked around me, his orange striped tail high in the air, sniffing. I was afraid he wouldn't remember me, but he got right up on his back legs and stretched his front legs against me to say hello.

Mrs. Fish and I carried the groceries down the hall. "Welcome to my home," Mrs. Fish said, after she put down her packages. She bowed and stretched out her arms. She rose on her toes, and I thought she looked like a huge, beautiful fairy godmother.

"Let me show you around, Joyce. Here's my kitchen." She pointed to the sink, stove, and fridge along one wall.

"My dining room." She touched the table and chairs.

"My animal room." There was a canary in a bamboo cage on a stand near one of the windows, and below it were beds for Greta and William. "Say hello to my darling Toot Sweet," Mrs. Fish said, sticking her finger into the cage. Toot Sweet cocked his head and whistled. "Yes, baby, yes," Mrs. Fish crooned.

In the middle of the room was a green velvet couch with a long table behind it, and smaller tables on each side. "My living room," Mrs. Fish said. "And my bedroom." She pointed to the couch again. "My parlor for the very best company." The couch again. "Well, there you have it."

She had everything she needed in that room—and much more. In our house if you wanted to see something you looked out the window. But in Mrs. Fish's house everywhere I looked there was something else to see. Calendars, candles, flowers and mugs, bowls and pictures, pencil holders stuffed with pencils with flowers on top and giant pens, boxes of writing paper and dolls and little stuffed bears and a whole row of china cats, and behind that another row of glass horses.

"Do you like my doodads?" Mrs. Fish asked, stroking a small gray stuffed rabbit. It had miniature pink ears and a little fuzzy white tail.

"I love them." I picked up a glass paperweight with a tiny evergreen tree in it, and under the tree an even tinier bird. I shook the paperweight. Snow swirled around the tree and the bird. I could have looked at it for hours, but I hurried on, picking up things and putting them down, trying to decide which was my favorite.

Finally I remembered Old Dad. I put down a cup with Snoopy on it and went to the window. The two long windows at the front of the room were both filled with all kinds of plants. So many plants that the windows and the canary in its cage looked like they were floating in green water. There were flowered curtains at the windows, and shades, and each shade had a long crocheted pull on it, and at the end of each pull was a little pink Hawaiian doll.

I looked down into the street. LT was parked in front of the market. "Mrs. Fish, Old Dad's here. I have to go." I hurried to the door.

Mrs. Fish came after me. "Joycie, why don't you and your Old Dad come up for some cake and tea?"

"He drinks coffee, Mrs. Fish."

"Then I'll make coffee." She scooped up William and looked over the railing as I ran down the stairs. It was already dark outside when I crossed to the market. I found Old Dad looking for me in the canned fish department. "Where you been?" he said.

We got the cart and stood in line. I told him about my visit to Mrs. Fish.

"Didn't I teach you not to go with strangers?"

"She works in school, Old Dad. She's not a stranger."

"Not blood kin."

"But Old Dad—"

"She's a stranger."

"Why do people have to be relatives?" I said.

"You want to trust them, they better be."

"I would trust Mrs. Fish with anything," I said.

"I never thought you were a fool."

That hurt my feelings. I didn't say anything else. We paid for our food and carried the groceries outside to LT.

"Yoo hooo . . . yooo hooooo!" Mrs. Fish leaned out her window. Her big round face looked like a moon floating in all those green leaves and vines. "Yoo hoo, Joycie, is that your Old Dad?" She waved to Old Dad, who was standing with his head flung back, looking up at her window.

"Who's that?" he said.

"Mrs. Fish."

"Hello, Old Dad," she called. "Joycie has told me all about you. Come up and have some refreshments."

Old Dad climbed into the truck. "Get in," he said. And the way he said it, I got in. But I rolled down the window so I could wave to Mrs. Fish.

Old Dad pulled away from the curb. The streets were dark. I looked at all the lighted windows and the people inside. "Mrs. Fish wanted to meet you," I said.

"No, she didn't."

"Yes, she did. She said so."

"People say things." He jutted his head forward and flattened his lips. "She don't want the Ape in her house."

"Don't say that. You're not an ape!"

Old Dad shrugged. "Depends who's looking."

"Mrs. Fish isn't like that. She's different. When you meet her, you'll see."

"Ain't gonna meet her." He had both hands on the steering wheel.

"Stubborn!" I said.

He gave me a sideways look. "Call me what you want. You just keep me out of this Mrs. Fish business." We drove the rest of the way home without talking.

❧ 9 ❧

Fish Business

"*Pssst!*" Mrs. Fish's round face peeked around a corner, her finger crooked at me. "Joycie," she whispered. It was as if we were spies, and the enemy was coming to get us. I slid around the corner, looking both ways. My heart was beating fast.

"Hello, Mrs. Fish," I whispered.

"Where are you going?" she said.

"To class."

"You'll be late."

"I know." I was moving slow on purpose.

Mrs. Fish pushed a broom around under the stairs. She was wearing her butterfly barrettes again.

"Come and have lunch with me today."

"Lunch?"

"Luncheon, dear one," Mrs. Fish said, smoothing down the stiff black whiskers on her chin. "Do you have any previous engagements?"

I shook my head. "I'll come!" I said. Then I remembered. "Thank you." I ran down the hall. I got to class just on time. All morning I watched the clock. School was better because I had something good to think about.

Just before lunchtime we went to art. I passed Lacey in the hall. She saw me, too. We just looked at each other.

At noon I carried my lunch bag down to Mrs. Fish's room. She had set the table with diamond-patterned paper plates and matching napkins. There were the same pretty artificial flowers in a green frog holder. There was a little dish of colored mints.

"Sit down, sit down," Mrs. Fish said. She put her red Roy Rogers lunch box on the table and took out two sandwiches. "What kind of sandwich do you have?" Mrs. Fish said.

"Swiss cheese," I said. "What's yours?"

"Chicken salad, and tuna fish. One for me, and one for you. Which do you choose?"

"I don't know. Mrs Fish. I always eat Swiss cheese."

"Always?"

"Yes. I love Swiss cheese."

"Oh, my. I wouldn't want to eat the same thing every day."

"I don't mind. I like it. I like things being the same."

"Still, you have to try something new once in a while. It adds a little spice to life. Now, me, I like to try new food, and new gadgets, and even new jobs once in a while. That's how I got this job. I got tired of my last one. I was working in a hospital. One day I just had enough of feeling sad about people. So I walked in here, and just like that, they hired me. Said their custodian had to have an operation and they didn't know when he'd be back. 'Well, Fish is your woman,' I said." She put her chicken salad sandwich on my plate. "You try that, and see if it isn't tasty."

"Won't you be hungry?" I put half my Swiss cheese on her plate.

"Sweet girl," she said.

My face got hot. I took a bite of chicken salad sandwich.

Mrs. Fish took chocolate chip cookies, two apples, and a box of Cheese Fritters from her lunch box. "Sharesies," she said, putting them in the middle of the table. I put my apple there, too.

"Isn't this lovely," Mrs. Fish said. "I would so much rather have company than eat alone. Ooops, excuse me, William. Of course you're good company, too."

The chicken salad sandwich was delicious. I kept taking bites and thinking of what she'd said to me. *Sweet girl.* "Mrs. Fish . . . did you mean that . . . about me being . . . sweet?"

"I certainly did. You're a very sweet girl. I noticed it right away. Why do you ask?"

"Nobody ever said it before, so I just wondered—"

"Oh, surely your mama said it to you many a time."

"I don't know. I don't remember." I told her about my mother. The real story, not the one I made up.

Mrs. Fish folded my hands in hers. "When I lost my mama I cried for a week."

William jumped into my lap and put one velvet paw on my face. I think he knew I felt like crying.

After we finished the food, we sucked on the mints. "This is just like a party," I said. "I'm having such a good time."

"Oh, no, parties are much better," Mrs. Fish said. "Mama always liked a party. She didn't care if she was giving a party, or someone was giving it for her, so long as it was a party. And I'm the same way. When was your last party?"

I shook my head. "I can't remember."

"Well, when's your birthday?"

"Not till March."

"What presents did you get? Presents can be just like a little party. You don't need a lot of people."

"Old Dad doesn't like presents," I said. "He says it's just a lot of junk that ends up in the dump."

"No birthday presents," Mrs. Fish said, looking shocked. "Someone should talk to your Old Dad."

"I don't mind," I said. I didn't want her to be mad at Old Dad. "He's just that way," I said. "If you knew him, you would understand. Anyway, I bet I had parties and presents when I lived with my mother."

"Of course you did." Mrs. Fish patted my hand. Her hand was big, fat, and warm. "I'm sure of that!" she said. Then the bell rang and I had to leave, but Mrs. Fish said I should come back again. "Any time," she said. "When can I expect you?"

I was worried it might not be polite to say the next day, so I said the day after. "Fine and dandy. I'll be looking for you, Joycie," she said.

I started eating lunch with Mrs. Fish almost every day. We talked about lots of things, about everything, Old Dad, and my mother, and the dump, and her family. One day she brought pictures to show. They were from a long time ago when she was Emily Fish. There was a picture of her with her hair in braids and ribbons and her arms full of kittens. There was another picture of her and her mother standing in front of their house. They had their arms around each other's waists. They were both fat and looking at each other with loving eyes.

"Wasn't Mama beautiful?" Mrs. Fish said. "We were so close, Joycie. We loved the same food, wore each other's clothes . . . laughed and cried at the same things. Mama often said we were the same soul in two bodies." Mrs. Fish stroked the picture of her mother. "Next time, Joycie, you bring some pictures."

"We don't have any," I said.

"Not even one of your dear mother?"

I shook my head. Mrs. Fish hugged me. "Dear one."

At home I was talking a lot about Mrs. Fish. I didn't think anything of it. I liked to tell Old Dad about the things in Mrs. Fish's room, and what we ate, and how William licked my fingers when he was feeling especially happy. "What does she want with you?" he said.

"She likes me."

"Everybody wants something. Basic rule."

"Not Mrs. Fish, Old Dad. She likes company for lunch. So do I."

"That's enough! You watch out for her. You don't know what people can do."

"Yes I do! But Mrs. Fish is different. She is, Old Dad! Mrs. Fish is *nice*."

"Nice, nice," he growled. "Every day now it's Fish this and Fish that, and Fish Fish Fish. I don't want to hear no more about this Fish business."

"All right! I won't ever talk about her again."

"That's what I said. Subject closed."

"What do you want to talk about then?"

"Nothing!" He didn't say one more word all evening. When I went up to bed, I said, "Good night!" but he just grunted. "Stubborn," I said.

The next day he still wasn't talking. He wasn't talking to anybody. It was Saturday, and all day in the dump, he only pointed, or shouted, or roared around on the dozer.

He had the miseries. He had them all weekend. On Sunday he didn't work on Face Pole. He didn't do anything, just sat in a chair by the window.

The next day I went to Mrs. Fish's room for lunch. I was thinking of asking her what to do to make Old Dad feel better. I was sure she'd know. But the moment I opened the door I forgot everything. Her little room was so full of light and color I thought the sun had burst inside it. I looked around, dazed. Mrs. Fish pulled me inside.

Clusters of yellow and orange balloons bobbed on the walls. Orange and yellow streamers crossed the ceiling. The table was covered with a yellow tablecloth, and there were orange and yellow cups and plates and napkins.

"What is it?" I said.

"It's a party," Mrs. Fish said. "Taa—daaa!" She flipped a yellow napkin up and under it I saw a cake, candles, white icing, and little silver dots spelling out HAPPY BIRTHDAY, JOYCE. My head swam. I didn't speak, because I didn't believe it.

"Happy birthday to you," Mrs. Fish sang. She held my hands and danced. "Happy birthday to you, dear Joycie, happy birthday to you!"

"But it's not my birthday," I said at last.

"Oh, tush! This is a surprise birthday-in-advance party. Come, let's eat our lunch."

She had brought all sorts of special things. Cream cheese and nut sandwiches cut in little triangles, fluted paper cups filled with chocolates and jelly beans, and ginger ale that we drank out of wine glasses.

We ate our sandwiches and drank our soda and nibbled the candy. William kept leaping up the walls, trying to catch the balloons. Every once in a while, a balloon burst with a loud *pop* and William leaped into the air in a frenzy.

When we finished eating, Mrs. Fish lit the candles on the cake. "Make a wish, then blow."

I closed my eyes, but I didn't know what to wish for. Then I remembered Old Dad. I wished that his miseries would go away, and he would feel good again. I took a breath and blew out all the candles.

"Your wish will come true," Mrs. Fish said. "Now cut the cake, Joycie, and give yourself the first slice."

"Thank you," I said. I wanted to say more, but I didn't know the words for it. "Thank you, Mrs. Fish."

"Not through yet," she said. She reached under the table and brought out a package wrapped in shiny yellow paper with a big white bow in one corner. "What's a birthday party without a birthday present?"

"For me?" I said. I could hardly breathe. I took off the bow and put it carefully to one side. I unwrapped the paper, and folded it. I loved the way it felt, so fresh and stiff. I opened the white box and pushed aside the tissue paper. Inside was a blouse embroidered around the collar and down the front with little blue and pink flowers. I had never seen anything so wonderful.

"Do you like it?" Mrs. Fish said. "You don't think there's too much embroidery, do you?"

"It's . . . perfect," I said. I covered the blouse with the tissue paper. "Mrs. Fish . . . Mrs. Fish . . ." I put my arms around her and hugged her. Then I thought of another wish I could have made. *Please . . . don't ever let Mrs. Fish go away.*

Ape House

"Attention, class." Mr. LaSorta rapped a ruler on his desk. "We're going to do some writing. Joyce. Sharon. Would you two please pass out these composition papers?"

I went up to the desk. "Here you are, girls," Mr. La-Sorta said. Sharon stood on the other side away from me. Mr. LaSorta was always asking Sharon and me to do things together. He had made Sharon and me the morning blackboard monitors. Maybe he thought we were best friends!

On the blackboard he wrote:

1. Three Things I Don't Like About Teachers.
2. My Best Friend's Worst Fault.
3. I Wish My Parents Would . . .

I finished passing out my stack of papers and sat down.

"All right, class," Mr. LaSorta said, "here's the ticket. Choose one topic and write me something really good. It doesn't have to be long, but make it something you feel"— he stabbed himself in the belly—"*right here*. Good handwriting. Don't forget tomorrow night is Parents' Night.

We'll put these compositions up for your folks to see."

The whole school was getting ready for Parents' Night. All the rooms were being cleaned up. The choir had been practicing songs. In gym we did tumbling, and the best tumblers were chosen for Parents' Night.

I studied the blackboard. I couldn't write about my best friend's worst fault because I didn't have a best friend. I couldn't write what I wished my parents would do because I didn't have parents. So I had to write three things I didn't like about teachers.

There are three things I don't like about teachers. I don't like it when a teacher feels sorry for a kid. No one should feel sorry for anyone. I don't mean you shouldn't feel bad if someone hurts themselves, but that's different. Feeling sorry means you think the kid has such a bad life. How do you know?

Another thing I don't like about teachers is when they act dumb. It's okay for a teacher not to know everything, but they should definitely know when kids are being sly or nasty. And the third thing I don't like about teachers is when they let kids play tricks on them. It's nice if a teacher laughs at something funny, but there are some things a teacher should not laugh about. What if a kid tore up important papers? Or went into the teacher's desk? Or another kid's desk? But mostly I like my teachers. I think they're very nice and pretty smart.

The next day Mr. LaSorta returned our compositions. He wrote on mine, "Very good, Joyce. Good thinking, and nice neat handwriting." He gave me an A with a circle around it. Then he had Sharon and me (the two of us, again!) collect all the papers and tack them up on the bulletin board at the back of the room. Sharon stayed as far away from me as she could, but we had to share the box of tacks.

"Don't get near me," she whispered fiercely. "You stink!" She punched a tack into the board.

"Finished, girls?" Mr. LaSorta smiled at us. Maybe he thought we were having a nice friendly talk.

We had a half-day because of Parents' Night. Just before dismissal Mr. LaSorta said, "Okay, I'll look forward to seeing all of you and your parents tonight. Let's make the best showing in the school, and all turn out. Raise your hands if you and your parents are coming."

Everyone raised their hands, except me. My face was hot. I thought of something else I should have written in my composition. *Another thing I don't like about teachers is when they embarrass kids.*

The bell rang. Everyone pushed back their chairs, and started talking and shoving to the door. Mr. LaSorta slowed people down. When I got to the door, he put his hand on my arm. "Got a minute, Joyce? You didn't raise your hand before. Aren't you coming tonight?"

"My Old Dad doesn't want to."

"Why not?"

"I don't know."

"Did he say so? What was his reason?"

Now I was really embarrassed. "Well . . . I just know that he doesn't want to."

"Joyce, you showed him the invitation, didn't you?"

I looked up at the ceiling. "No," I said at last.

Mr. LaSorta smoothed his mustache. "That's not cricket, Joyce."

"Old Dad never comes," I said quickly. "So it would have been just a waste of time to ask him."

"Well, I'm really sorry. I was looking forward to meeting your father."

"He's not my father. He's my uncle."

"Your uncle, then. I'd like to meet him. I'd like to tell him what a good student you are."

"I am?" I was as surprised as when Mrs. Fish told me I was sweet.

"You are. You know, Joyce, I have a daughter, not as big as you, yet. Her name is Andrea."

"That's a pretty name." I imagined Mr. LaSorta and his wife and his little girl all sitting together on a couch. Mrs. LaSorta had long straight black hair, and Andrea had curls. The LaSorta Family At Home. It was like a picture.

"Every Saturday Andrea and I go out together," Mr. LaSorta said. "We shop, or we play ball, or we take a walk. Do you do things with your uncle?"

"We shop, too," I said. "And in winter we feed the deer." I was glad I could say those things. We didn't just work in the dump. But, still, we weren't a real family like the LaSortas.

"Would you promise me something, Joyce? Tell your uncle about Parents' Night and ask him to come. I'm sure he will. When Andrea goes to school I won't want to miss her Parents' Night."

I could have told him that was different. But he was looking at me in a way that made me nod and say I'd try.

When I got home I checked the mailbox. Empty. I shut the door, and that's when I noticed that someone had chalked in big red letters on the side of the box: THE APE LIVES HERE.

I spit on my fingers and rubbed it off as best I could. Why did people think they could call Old Dad anything? He never hurt anybody. Just because he was sort of short and looked different. Just because he wasn't handsome like Mr. LaSorta.

I started up the road. A car passed me going out. A woman was driving. She waved to me. What if she was the one who'd written THE APE LIVES HERE on our mailbox? It could be her. It could be anyone. Old Dad always said you couldn't trust anyone except your family. Was he right? I trusted Mr. LaSorta, and Mrs. Fish. I was sure I could tell Mrs. Fish *anything*.

While we were eating supper I said, "Old Dad? Guess what?"

"Guess what, what?" he said, spreading mustard on his hot dog.

"It's Parents' Night tonight." I mixed my baked beans with bits of bread. "You want to go?"

"You want me to?" he said.

I didn't expect that answer. I thought he'd just say, *No*, and that would be that. I gulped down some milk. I would like Old Dad to meet Mr. LaSorta. And how about Mrs. Fish? She was going to be in school. I could get them to really meet each other at last. But I was worried, too. What if someone made a garbage joke and Old Dad heard it? Or said something about the Ape in the Ape House?

"It's up to you," I said.

"What do *you* want?" he said.

"I don't know."

"Huh! You don't want me to go." He put his bowl in the sink and turned on the water. There was a look on his face, closed up, that I called his blind look. It meant his feelings were hurt, but he wasn't letting on. "I bet that Fish is going to be there," he said. "Maybe you want to go with her."

"Old Dad, you never go to those Parents' Night things."

He dried his bowl and put it away. "Who's going to be

there? Everybody?" I nodded. "Kids you go to school with?"

"Yes."

"Teachers, principals, all of them?"

"Yes."

"Okay. We're going."

"We're *going?*"

"You heard me."

"You never went before."

"Always a first time," he said.

"Old Dad!" I hugged him. "Guess what, I've got a paper up on the board, and—"

"Okay, okay, you're choking me. Let's go if we're going."

"You have to change into good clothes."

"Think I don't know that?"

"Well, I'm just telling you," I said.

"Take care of yourself," he said. "I'll take care of Henry."

"Henery Fenery," I yelled, running up the stairs. "Beat you changing."

When I came down wearing my new blouse Old Dad was ironing his shirt. He spit on his finger to test the iron, then slammed it down on the sleeve.

"You're going to burn a hole in it," I said.

"You got something to say about everything, Joyce."

"Guess who taught me!" I was really feeling glad. But on the way to school I got a little nervous again.

"I'll talk to your main teacher first," Old Dad said. He drove with both hands on the wheel, looking very serious. He was wearing blue pants, a white shirt, and his good shoes shined up. He'd shaved, and dunked his head in water before he combed his hair. "How do I look?" he said.

"You look handsome!" I said proudly.

School was packed with people. All the lights were on. The floors were shining. I saw RB, and his sister Bubba, and their mother. I saw Michael Stacey, and that little boy, Steven. Then I saw Lacey with a woman who looked just like her. Same long brown hair, same brown eyes. Even her front teeth stuck out a little like Lacey's. Lacey looked at me, then at Old Dad.

I don't know why, but suddenly I called, "Lacey! This is my Old Dad," I said. "Is that your mother?" Oh, how stupid! My face burned. What if Lacey didn't answer me?

Lacey bit her lip. She looked at me. Then she touched her mother's arm. "Mom, this is . . . Joyce." Her mother smiled at me. That was all. It wasn't anything, but—I don't know why—it made me feel so great!

Sharon and Linda were monitoring at my classroom. They stared at Old Dad. "Hello!" I said. "This is my uncle, Mr. Adams!"

"Welcome to Parents' Night," Sharon said, sounding as if someone wound her up.

Linda handed Old Dad a pencil and pad. "Please sign in." She rolled her eyes at Sharon. Maybe she thought Old Dad couldn't write his name! When we walked into the room I accidentally on purpose stepped on Sharon's toes.

Mr. LaSorta was talking to some people, so we had to wait. I showed Old Dad my composition on the bulletin board. "That's your paper, huh?" Old Dad read it, his lips moving.

"This is my girl's paper," he said, turning to a man. His voice was too loud for the classroom. "See that A there, she got an A!" People in front turned. Sharon and Linda peered around, giving each other sly looks. I wished I'd stepped harder on Sharon's toes.

When it was our turn Mr. LaSorta held out his hand. "Mr. Adams?"

"Mr. LaSorta?" Old Dad said, just as loud as before. He shook Mr. LaSorta's hand.

"I'm Joyce's teacher."

"I'm her uncle!"

"Very glad you came, Mr. Adams."

"That's okay," Old Dad said. "I don't mind."

"Joyce is a good student."

"She's smart," Old Dad said, nodding.

"Sometimes she daydreams a little, but that's not so bad."

"I'll talk to her," Old Dad said.

They shook hands again. We walked out. I was proud of Old Dad! I liked the way he talked to Mr. LaSorta. Then I saw Mrs. Fish. She was wearing a long flowered dress. She had her butterfly barrettes tucked into her big cloud of gray hair. She was wearing an armful of bracelets, and necklaces and chains. She looked big, fat, strong, and beautiful.

"Mrs. Fish!" I waved to her. "There's Mrs. Fish, Old Dad."

"Let's go, let's go," Old Dad said.

"No, Old Dad. We have to say hello to Mrs. Fish."

Mrs. Fish came toward us. "There you are," she called out in her high voice. "Joycie, you look beautiful." She held out her hands.

"It's the blouse," I said, squeezing her hands.

"It fits you just right," Mrs. Fish said. "And *so* becoming." She turned to Old Dad. She was way taller than him. "Mr. Adams, I bet you don't even remember me. I'm the girl who waved to you from the window. So, we meet at last. How do you do?"

Old Dad touched her hand and looked away. " 'Lo," he said.

"How do you like our school, Mr. Adams?" Mrs. Fish said. "We all have been working hard to get ready for Parents' Night. I mopped and waxed all these floors today with my own little hands."

I hated the way she was talking, high, fast, and giggly. But even more I hated the way Old Dad had his mouth clamped shut and his eyes almost closed from scowling so hard.

I looked away and in a glass door I saw the three of us reflected. I saw me in the middle, skinny and gloomy. I saw Old Dad standing to one side a mile wide with his sloping shoulders and barrel chest. I saw Mrs. Fish, ever so tall, and fat, and smiling hard. We looked like three freaks!

Like three people who had bumped into one another and didn't know how to get untangled. We looked like we all came from different planets. Where did I ever get the idea that Mrs. Fish and Old Dad would like each other?

❧ 11 ❧

Dancing Shoes

"Cold this morning," I said, sitting down at the table with my cereal. Old Dad had on his black winter cap with the earlaps turned up. He'd built a fire in the wood-burning stove.

"You going to see her today?" He looked at me sideways.

"Who?"

"*Her.*"

"You mean Mrs. Fish? I hope so."

"What're you going to do?"

"Nothing, just eat lunch."

He tipped up his saucer and drank the coffee that had spilled over. "Why?"

"Why what, Old Dad?"

"Hey! Don't talk to me like that."

"What?" I was so startled I dropped my spoon.

"Don't pretend. You know what I mean."

"Old Dad, what's the matter with you?"

"Ain't nothing the matter with *me.*" His forehead was

74

scrunched into deep lines. I could hardly see his eyes. "I asked you something."

"What?"

"Why you eat lunch with her all the time!"

"Because she's nice, and she's fun. And something else, she doesn't yell at me like you do. She has nice manners!"

He shoved back his chair. "She tell you to say that to me?" He grabbed his jacket and stomped to the door.

"No, she didn't, and you don't have to be so disagreeable," I said.

The door slammed. I put my dish in the sink and got my jacket. There was a tight bad feeling in my chest. All day it got worse. I couldn't understand why Old Dad and I were fighting.

When I got off the bus at the end of the day I didn't even stop to look in our mailbox. I walked down the road and into the dump. It was empty. I didn't see Old Dad. I called him, my voice echoing back from the trees.

"Old Dad!" I shouted. Suddenly I was sure something awful had happened. I was being punished for being so mean to him this morning. "Old Dad! Old Dad!"

He walked out of the work shack. I felt dizzy with relief. "You're here," I said, running up to him. I put my arm through his and pressed my face against his sleeve.

"Where'd you think I'd be?"

"I was so worried . . . because we had a fight . . . and we didn't make up."

"What fight?" he said.

"The one we had this morning."

"I wasn't fighting," he said. "Maybe you were."

"Yes, you were! This morning . . . you were mad at me."

"Not me," he said.

"Stubborn!"

"Hey, you going to help me? Or you going to stand around and gab all afternoon? There's papers over there gotta be bundled."

After we closed up and went back to the house, I made cheese-and-onion omelets. I toasted a big stack of bread and spread it with apple butter, and made a fresh pot of coffee. Three things Old Dad especially liked.

"Good," he said when he finished eating. He pushed away his plate. "How do you like my new shoes?" he said. He stood up and flapped around the room in a pair of enormous white shoes. They were ten times too big for Old Dad. A giant must have brought them to the dump.

"When did you put *those* on?" I said. "I didn't see you put them on."

"Think you see everything?" He kicked one leg high in the air, clapped his foot down, then danced around the room with his knees bent like an ape, scratching under his arms and smacking his lips.

"Old Dad . . . don't! You're making my stomach hurt!" I couldn't stop laughing.

"Hey! You think these shoes are too fancy for me? Wrong! These shoes fit me perfect. They're dancing shoes," he said. And before I knew it he'd taken my hand and started swinging me around the room.

Slaaap went the white shoes. *Slaaap . . . slaaap . . . slaaaaap. . . .*

Round and round we went. Old Dad's face got red as a balloon, and his little blue eyes gleamed like pieces of sky. "We're dancing," I cried, "we're dancing!"

"Slow down," he said. "I'm getting dizzy." He staggered around the room and fell into a chair.

"You okay?" I threw my arms around his neck and hugged him.

He waved me off. "It's passing. . . . Never mind. Hey! What're we gonna do with these shoes?"

"I'll keep them," I said, and I took them upstairs with me and hung them on the wall.

The next day when I got to the dump, I saw a man throwing bags full of garbage on the ground.

"Mister! Don't dump your garbage there," I said. I pointed to the pit. "In the hole."

Old Dad wasn't in the work shack, or the open sheds. The dozer was by the sand hill. On the bench outside the work shack, Old Dad's thermos was open, his lunch uneaten. I went back and looked over the edge of the ravine. He wasn't there. He wasn't anywhere around. "Old Dad?" I called.

I found him on the road to the house, face down in the dirt. I thought he was dead. "Old Dad!" I shook him frantically and tried to turn him over. He stirred, but he didn't turn. I got down on my knees and pushed and shoved. When I got him turned over he just lay there, panting, his face twisted to one side.

"Help . . . me. . . ." Tears were leaking from one eye. "Don't look . . . Joyce. . . ." He sucked in his lips and groaned. "Something . . . bad . . . with me. . . ."

He couldn't move his left arm and there was something wrong with his left leg. I got his good arm over my shoulder and hung on to it with both hands. He pushed up with his good leg. I got him halfway up, then we went down.

"Again . . ." he whispered, "try again. . . ."

I got him up again. We moved a couple of steps, then he slipped. I hung on desperately as he slid down to a sitting position. My face, my arms, my hands were wet with sweat. I was terrified. I looked into his face. His eyes were pleading. I pulled him up again. He staggered a few steps, then he had to rest. He was shaking. We went that way, a couple of steps at a time, till we got to our house. It had taken a long time. I got him into the house and onto the bed. Then he just lay there groaning and breathing through his mouth. I knelt down on the floor and leaned against the bed.

After a while, his good hand came down on top of my head. "Saved . . . me," he said. "Good . . . girl."

I held his hand against my face and cried.

12

The Ape Is Crying

Old Dad lay on his bed, tears running down his face. "The Ape . . . is crying," he said. "Funny . . . don't pay no attention. . . . Joyce, I'm trying to laugh, but . . . everything coming out backwards. . . ."

"Old Dad. Old Dad." I wiped his face with a corner of my shirt. It was morning. Rain streamed down the windows. "I'm going to go for a doctor!"

"No!"

"Why not? You're sick."

"No! No doctor!" He thrashed around. Last night was the same thing. As soon as I said "doctor," he got very upset. I looked at the clock. Time for the school bus. Past time to open the gate. Old Dad's eyes followed mine. He heaved himself up with his good hand so he was half-sitting, then he fell back. "Can't . . . no doctor, Joyce!"

"Okay, Old Dad! No doctor." I covered him with a blanket. "Don't worry about the dump. I'm going to do it. You rest." I kissed him and started tiptoeing away.

His eyes opened. "Joyce! Don't . . . tell! Don't tell I'm sick. *Promise.*"

79

I nodded. He made me say it. "I promise not to tell!"

I went into the kitchen. "What should I do first?" I was talking to myself. My stomach gurgled. I'd forgotten to eat last night. Was it bad to be hungry when Old Dad was sick?

I thought about school . . . the gate . . . garbage . . . Old Dad . . . food. . . . Everything jumped around in my mind. The clock ticked loudly. *Tick tick tick tick tick tick.* I couldn't stop it ticking. The gate had to be opened. Old Dad should eat. He needed food, he needed rest. Why wouldn't he let me get a doctor? Was he going to get better? What if he died?

I ate, but I didn't know what I ate. I put on my slicker, Old Dad's rain hat and my rubber boots. The road was half-mud. At the gate I found three bags of garbage. Maybe people would stay home because of the weather.

But all morning cars and trucks drove in with their lights on. I pushed the stuff over the edge of the ravine. When a woman asked for Old Dad, I just shrugged. "Think he'll be back soon?" I shook my head. "Cat got your tongue?" she said.

Around noon I sat down in the work shack. I'd forgotten to bring food. It was damp inside the shack. I built a fire, but then I had to go outside again and the fire went out. Cars and trucks drove in. They kept coming and coming. The dump was a muddy mess. I worked all day; I was afraid to stop working. But hard as I worked I couldn't keep up with things.

When it was dark, I locked up and went back to the house. Old Dad was sleeping on his bed with his mouth open. I shook him awake.

"How do you feel, Old Dad?"

"Bad," he groaned.

I gave him juice, and helped him to the bathroom, then back to his bed. Afterward I opened a can of soup. I ate it cold from the can. I boiled an egg for Old Dad. I got him propped up in his bed and tried to feed him the egg. He pushed away my hand and fed himself with his good hand. I put my head on my arms just for a second and fell asleep at the table. When I woke up, I heard Old Dad snoring. I damped the fire in the stove, then staggered upstairs. *Please*, I thought, as I fell into bed, *please, make Old Dad better . . . please . . . please. . . .*

13

What Are We Going To Do?

Old Dad pulled himself slowly around the house, holding on to furniture with his good hand and dragging his bad leg behind him. Every day he was just a little better, but at night when he was tired, tears leaked out of his eyes.

He was afraid the county people would take away his job, if they knew. He was afraid they'd take me away. I had never seen Old Dad afraid before. Every day he made me promise I wouldn't tell anyone about his sickness. "Swear, Joyce," he said. I raised my hand. "I swear, Old Dad!"

In the morning I got up early, made cereal and helped Old Dad out of bed. After I ate, I got my jacket and the keys and went to the dump. All the time I worked I worried about Old Dad alone in the house. Lunchtime I went back to see him. I worried about him, but he worried about the dump. I kept telling him everything was fine, but the truth was the garbage was piling up and piling up.

One day I decided I had to try the dozer. I'd watched

Old Dad at work lots of times. When nobody was around I got up in the seat, put in the key, turned on the switch, and threw in the clutch. The dozer jolted off like a rabbit.

I turned off the switch fast. When I got my breath back I started it again. I backed it against the sand bank, then moved it forward a little, then back again. Up and back, up and back, till I could do it smoothly. Next, I started raising and lowering the scoop. While I was doing this a car drove in. My heart jumped, but the people dumped their garbage and left without even looking at me.

All day I practiced on the dozer, and the next day I began pushing garbage into the pit. I dug into the hill, up for a load of sand, and covered over the garbage. I turned off the motor, stood up, and looked at what I'd done. Not as good as Old Dad's work, and a lot slower, but I was doing it!

All week cars came in and out. People dumped their garbage. Nobody asked me anything. They looked at me, didn't see Old Dad . . . but they didn't say *boo!* And neither did I. It was what Old Dad wanted. But sometimes I felt crazy, I wanted to yell and scream: *Old Dad is sick. Doesn't anybody care?*

Eleven days after I found Old Dad on the path I went back to school. Old Dad told me to. I didn't want to go. I didn't want to leave him alone all day. He still couldn't work.

"I want to stay home," I said. "Who's going to take care of the dump?"

Old Dad was buttoning his shirt with one hand. His left hand was no good for anything. I had tied it up in a scarf knotted around his neck so it wouldn't just hang. He held on to a chair, then a table, and shuffled into the kitchen. He was putting some weight on his left leg. He filled the kettle, then put it on the stove. Everything with one hand.

"Let me stay home just one more day."

"No! You go to . . . books." He banged his hand on the wall. Sometimes he said the wrong word, and then he'd get mad at himself. "Books," he said hoarsely. "No! Bo . . . sss . . . sss . . . school! You go to school!"

In school, everything looked too bright, glary. Voices sounded too sharp. I couldn't stop thinking about the dump and Old Dad. Mr. LaSorta asked if I'd been sick.

I shook my head, then quickly nodded yes. My face was hot. I was afraid he knew I was lying. "I missed you," he said. "Are you sure everything is okay?" I nodded. "Bring a note tomorrow from your uncle," he said.

Every day I went to school. I didn't talk to anyone. I didn't visit Mrs. Fish. I was afraid to. Afraid I'd tell her everything. When I saw her in the hall I turned and went the other way. It made me feel so bad.

One afternoon Lacey came into the cafeteria just after I sat down. She sat down at a table near me. We looked at each other. I started unwrapping my sandwich.

"Swiss cheese?" Lacey said.

I looked up. "What?" Was she talking to me?

"I *said*, Are you still eating Swiss cheese for lunch?"

"Uh-huh." I took a bite.

"Aren't you sick of it?" She was eating a submarine.

"No, I like it."

"I hate eating the same thing all the time."

She was really talking to me. I was so surprised I didn't know what to say. I wanted to say something friendly, but I was afraid to be too friendly.

"I haven't seen you in school for a while," Lacey said.

"I haven't been in school."

"Sick?"

"Sort of."

Just then Sharon and Linda came in. They were both wearing green shirts. They walked past Lacey and sat down at another table. Lacey acted as though she didn't even see them.

"Lacey," Linda called. "Oh, Lacey."

Lacey turned. Linda and Sharon put their thumbs in their mouths and sucked loudly. Lacey's face turned bright red. She looked ready to cry. I wanted to yell over to her, *Don't let them know they're making you feel bad!*

But I didn't say it. I didn't say anything. Because now I knew why Lacey had been so friendly to me! She didn't really like me. She just had a fight with Sharon and Linda. I got up and passed by her table. She didn't look up. Her eyes were down. She wasn't looking at anyone.

Every day when I jumped off the bus I ran down our road as fast as I could. Even though I knew better, I listened for the dozer. *Maybe Old Dad is better . . . so good that he's working. . . .* I ran into the dump. Empty. A blackbird sitting on top of a tree whistled. Plastic garbage bags covered the ground. Flies buzzed around rotting trash. Papers, plastic, chairs, boxes, and old tires littered the whole place. I hated it. It was ugly and evil. It didn't look like Old Dad's dump.

I kicked a broken chair out of my way. In the work shack flies buzzed against the windows. I pulled on gloves and charged out. I wanted to do everything! I wanted to clear away all the garbage, cover it over, stack the papers, push aside the metal, pile up the tires. But I was like one of those flies buzzing at the window. I went here and there, but when it got dark the dump was still trashy, it still smelled evil.

Old Dad was waiting for me in the house. "You're late."

"I was working in the dump."

He dragged around the room using a thick stick I'd found for him. "Got to get back to work."

"You will, Old Dad."

"When?" he demanded, pounding the stick.

"I don't know. You will, Old Dad. You're getting better every day."

With his good hand he worked the fingers of his bad hand. I didn't tell him how awful the dump was. I was tired. My head hurt. I had too many secrets.

Old Dad had made a pot of spaghetti for supper. I was almost too tired to eat. I dumped in butter and cheese, and we sat down and ate the spaghetti out of the pot. I leaned on my hand. What if I *had* said something to Lacey today when Linda and Sharon were teasing her? If I had a phone, I could call her right now. *This is your ex-old-best-friend calling. I just wanted to tell you I think Sharon Mason and Linda Justice are real dopes. Too bad I didn't punch them out for you today. You are one hundred percent nicer than either of them!*

Then Lacey would say, *Joyce, we should be best friends again.* After that I'd tell her about Old Dad and make her swear not to tell anyone. And she'd say, *Didn't you even tell Mrs. Fish he's sick? Joyce, you have to tell Mrs. Fish . . . Mrs. . . . Fish . . . Fishhhh. . .*

"Joyce! Hey! Joyce!"

My head jerked up. I'd fallen asleep at the table. "Are you okay, Old Dad?"

"Take this thing off." He pointed to the scarf holding up his arm. I undid the knot at the back of his neck. His arm flopped down. I moved it up, and down, and sideways. My arm got tired. "More," he said. "Keep it up. Make it move!"

"You feel anything this time?"

"Not yet. Keep moving it."

A few mornings later when we were eating our cereal, Old Dad said he was going to work in the dump. "How can you?" I said. His left arm just hung by his side. He still dragged his left leg.

"I'm going," he said, pushing out his lips. His face was different since he'd gotten sick. Everything on the left side was lower than on the right side.

It was a gray morning. I packed lunches for both of us while Old Dad got dressed. It took a long time for him to do everything. I put his cap on his head. Then we went down the road together, Old Dad leaning on me hard.

When we got to the dump, he looked all around. I thought he would yell and swear, but he didn't say a word, just looked at everything.

I made a fire in the work shack and put Old Dad's lunch and thermos on the table. "You'll be okay here?" I said.

"Not staying here," Old Dad said. "I gotta keep an eye on things. You come help me up on the crusher. . . . No! I mean the . . . the . . ."

"The *dozer*?" I said.

"That's it, the dozer."

"You can't run the dozer!"

Old Dad shuffled to the door, leaning heavily on his stick. "You gonna help me, Joyce?"

It wasn't easy getting him up on the dozer with that bad leg. I pushed and he pulled with his good arm. When he was finally on the seat his face dripped sweat. He put his good right hand on the wheel. He was wearing his red-and-black work jacket. I put his left hand in the pocket. "How do I look?" he said.

"You look good, you look really good, but Old Dad—"

"Get going," he said.

"Let me stay home today," I said. "Just today, so I can help you out."

"Don't you miss that bus!" I didn't want to go, but he made me.

At noon I was on my way to the cafeteria when Mrs. Fish stopped me. "Hello, Joyce."

"Hello, Mrs. Fish." I was so glad to see her my voice cracked.

"My friend hasn't visited me in weeks," she said. "I've missed her."

"I just couldn't—" I could feel everything spilling into my mouth, all the things I wanted to tell her. "I'm sorry I . . . I"

"Tush! Don't be sorry. Can you come to lunch today?"

I shook my head.

"Sure now?" she said.

"No, no, I can't." I knew I could never keep Old Dad's secret if I went to her room.

"Oh, well . . ." She giggled and twirled her fingers. "Cha-cha-cha, I just thought I'd ask my favorite lunch friend." There were two big bright red spots on her cheeks.

My throat filled up. I'd hurt her feelings. I didn't know what to say. There was nothing to say! I walked away, out the door. I left school. A cold hard rain was falling. *Old Dad, why'd you make me promise? Old Dad!* — The rain was like a gray sheet covering everything. I thought of Old Dad up on the dozer. Was he still sitting there? I began to run.

In the dump I found Old Dad, half on the dozer, half on the ground, caught like an animal in a trap. His bad leg was jammed under the seat. His cap was lying in a puddle.

I pulled him up. I didn't feel his weight. I didn't feel

anything. Something happened to me. I just raised Old Dad and walked him back to the house as if I was the strongest person in the world.

In the house I turned on the lights and built up the fire. I got dry clothes for Old Dad. I changed my clothes. I made hot milk and opened a box of crackers and put cheese on the table. I did everything calmly, but inside me, my heart wanted to fly out of my body.

One day I said, "Please, Old Dad, don't go to the dump."

"You want me to sit here all day like a lump of mud?" He struggled into his jacket. His eyes were little, angry and sad at the same time.

"Then let me stay home," I said.

"No! You want them to come . . . those people . . . keepers . . . you know who I mean! County . . . you want them to take you away?" He lurched to the door.

I helped him up on the dozer again. I didn't want him to sit there, but he said he *had* to. "I tell 'em to put their garbage in the right place, and they listen to me up here."

All morning in school, I had a hard time paying attention. Mr. LaSorta kept looking at me. I was thinking about Old Dad. What if he fell off the dozer again? What if his arm and leg never got better? *What are we going to do?* It was a shout inside my head. *What are we going to do?* The shout got louder. It got so loud I thought my head might burst.

When the bell rang I rushed out of the room, down the hall and down the stairs. "Mrs. Fish!" I called in front of her door. "Mrs. Fish! Mrs. Fish!"

She opened the door. She was wearing her railroad overalls, holding a half-eaten apple in her hand.

"Mrs. Fish," I cried. "Oh, Mrs. Fish. What are we going to do?"

14

Bump on a Log

"What are we going to do, Mrs. Fish?"

She drew me into her room. "Sit down, dear one, calm yourself." William jumped into my lap. He was warm, but I couldn't stop shivering.

"Now tell me," Mrs. Fish said, taking my hands.

"It's Old Dad." My throat tightened. "Oh, Mrs. Fish!"

"Is something wrong with your Old Dad?" I nodded. "Is he sick?"

"He . . . fell," I said. "I think he fell. His leg . . . and his arm . . . his hand . . . They don't move. His arm just hangs there, Mrs. Fish. Like it's dead." I thought I would tell her just a little, but then I couldn't stop myself. I told her everything. About staying out of school, about the dump getting so awful, and Old Dad's falling off the dozer in the rain.

"Oh, my! We have to think," Mrs. Fish said. "First, we'll have some hot tea."

I had talked so much that I felt empty and light, like the brown papery cicada cases I found in the summer that you could crush with one pinch of your fingers.

Mrs. Fish handed me a cup of tea. I blew on it. The steam went into my face, and then my eyes got wet.

Mrs. Fish folded her hands together under her chin. "Your Old Dad needs a doctor," she said. "That's the first thing. I believe he's had a small stroke."

"He won't go to a doctor," I said. "He's afraid about his job, and me."

"Hmmm . . . yes. . . ." She dipped her pinkie into her tea. "Things like that have been known to happen. So, let's think again."

I stroked William. It was good to have someone else worrying and thinking for me. "Old Dad can't work, Mrs. Fish. And I can't do it all alone. I try. When I stayed home it was better."

Mrs. Fish patted my hand. "No staying home. You and I will work in the dump. You'll show me what to do, and together we'll do it."

I thought of her mops and buckets and her big metal waste cart on wheels. The dump was different. A lot different. "But, Mrs. Fish—"

"No buts," she said. "You can look for me bright and early on Saturday. We'll be a super-duper team!"

Saturday morning I was up early. Outside the ground was white with frost, but the sun was shining. Mrs. Fish was coming, and I still hadn't told Old Dad.

Downstairs he sat on the side of his bed, twisted around trying to put on his green work shirt. His bad arm was in the sleeve, but the rest of the shirt was bunched up behind him.

"You want help?" I said.

Grunting, he grabbed the shirt in his good hand and yanked it around. "Make breakfast," he said. "I'll take care of my own dressing."

In the kitchen I fried bread in lard and cut in our last onion. We hadn't shopped since Old Dad got sick, and we were running out of everything. I made coffee and opened a can of condensed milk. I fixed cracker-and-bologna sandwiches for lunch. The bologna was going green at the edges, but I cut off those parts.

While we were eating, I said, "Old Dad? Remember Mrs. Fish?"

He looked at me over his coffee cup. His left arm was lying in his lap. "Just because my arm's dead don't mean my brain's dead, too. What about the Fish?" He stared at his hand, at the fingers just lying there doing nothing. And watching him, seeing his face twist, I felt so bad I couldn't say a word.

"Nothing. Forget it," I said. I washed my dishes and put them away. "Can I wear your big hat?" I said.

"It ain't raining."

"I just like to wear it."

He waved his hand. "Okay. Where's the keys? Let's go."

"We're going to really get some things done today," I said on the way to the dump. "I'll drive the dozer—"

"You ain't driving no dozer."

"Yes, I am. We have to cover the garbage in the pit—"

"You're not old enough."

"I know how to do it, Old Dad."

"Somebody catches you, it's me they're going to tear apart."

"I won't use it when anyone's around!"

"I'll think about it," he said, and I had to be satisfied with that. But at least when we got to the dump, he didn't make me help him up on the dozer. He sat down on the bench outside the work shack where he could watch everything.

I went down the road to unlock the gate. Mrs. Fish was already there in her car. "Good morning," she called, leaning out the window. "Isn't this some morning!"

When we got to the dump I got out first. Old Dad called me. "Joyce! Come here."

"Oh, my," Mrs. Fish said, as she looked around at the garbage and flies. "Oh, my." She waved her hands above her head. "Shoo! Shoo!"

"Mrs. Fish came to help us, Old Dad," I said.

Old Dad pounded his stick on the ground. "We don't need no help."

"Old Dad—"

"Tell her to go home."

"You can trust her. She won't tell about you being sick, Old Dad. The dump is awful, we need her—"

"Get her the holy h-hell out of here," Old Dad roared.

Mrs. Fish's chin stiffened. "You're a sick man. It's nothing to be ashamed of. We can all use a little help now and then—"

Old Dad beat his good hand on his thigh. "I never took nothing from nobody."

"I'm not giving *you* anything," Mrs. Fish said. "I'm doing it for Joyce. The child has too much on her." She crossed her arms. "Why don't you just tell me what to do."

I held my breath. I'd never seen anybody stand up to Old Dad.

He turned his head, chewing on his lip something fierce. Then he jerked his thumb. "Let her sort trash, Joyce!"

"Come on, Mrs. Fish," I said quickly. I just had time to show her around when the cars started coming and we went to work. From the bench, Old Dad kept his eye on everything.

A man on a truck filled with brush called, "How about some help, Henry?"

"Help yourself!" Old Dad yelled.

I jumped on the back of the truck. The man and I shoved the brush over the edge of the ravine. "What's the matter, the old guy taking it easy?" the man said.

I worked faster. I was sweating. I glanced over my shoulder. Mrs. Fish was working hard, too. Old Dad was yelling at everyone to dump their trash in the right place.

All morning we kept so busy we didn't have a chance to talk till after noon when things quieted down and we stopped for lunch.

Mrs. Fish pulled a little mirror out of one of her pockets. "Oh, my!" Her face was streaky dirty. "Where's the little girls' room, Joycie?"

"At the house." I pointed her down the road.

As soon as she was out of sight, Old Dad said, "Nothing good is gonna come of this. She wants something. You don't get nothing for free in this world. Basic rule."

"She's just nice," I said, handing him crackers and bologna.

"You wait and see," he said in his stubborn voice.

"Oh, I can't talk to you when you're like this!"

"Then don't talk to me," he said. "Go on, go to the little girls' room."

"She was just trying to be polite," I said. "Polite people don't say toilet."

Old Dad snorted. Just then we heard Mrs. Fish coming down the path, whistling. "Whistling females," Old Dad muttered, "and wet hens, they come to no good ends."

"Old Dad, I whistle all the time."

"That's different."

"Here I am," Mrs. Fish called. I loved the way she

moved, big and smooth, like she was on wheels. She sat down next to me. The bench creaked, and I moved over to make more room for her, but not too far. It was so nice sitting right next to her. And even better having her on one side of me and Old Dad on the other side.

Mrs. Fish put her lunch box on her knees. "Mmm, bologna," she said, looking into our lunch bag. "Isn't that nice. What else do you have?"

"That's it." I dug out some cracker crumbs. "We haven't had time to cook so much."

Mrs. Fish brought out a thick turkey sandwich. "I can't eat all this food, Joycie. You'll have to help me." She passed me half her sandwich, then peered around me at Old Dad. "Working here is just like cleaning house. A place for everything, and everything in its place. Don't you think so, Mr. Adams?"

Old Dad flapped his good hand. "Tell her," he said to me, "if she thinks it's like cleaning a house, she's got bats in her belfry."

"Old Dad!" I was really mad at him.

He shuffled into the work shack and then out again. "Can't sit like a bump on a log all day," he said. He started stacking paper with his good hand. After lunch I got on the dozer and pushed garbage into the pit. For a while Old Dad watched me work. "Don't be a cowboy!" he yelled. I was very careful. I didn't do anything fast or dangerous. I moved lots of garbage, but more kept coming in.

At the end of the day Mrs. Fish asked what time we opened on Sunday. Her overalls had grease stains. Her hair was coming out of her scarf.

"Tell her we don't open on Sunday," Old Dad said. "Tell her it's our day off."

"You tell him you've been working Sundays, and he knows it," Mrs. Fish said.

"You tell her that's different! I don't want her to come. I can't pay."

"Who wants his money?" Mrs. Fish said. "You tell him I'll be here tomorrow morning, eight o'clock sharp."

15

Tapping Fingers

Old Dad and I had oatmeal for Sunday breakfast, and I hard-boiled the last two eggs for our lunch. On the back of the shelf I found a can of baked beans and we took that, too. We were out of everything.

At eight o'clock Mrs. Fish drove in, honking her horn. "Here I am!"

Everything was the same as the day before, except that no new garbage piled up. By the end of the day the dump looked better than it had in weeks. The smell and the flies were gone. We had piled wood, stacked metal, put bottles into the bottle bin and rags into plastic bags. Mrs. Fish and I wheeled two old refrigerators and a washer to one of the open sheds, and Old Dad checked them over while we kept working.

Late in the day Mrs. Fish found a chair with a split leg that someone had thrown on the brush pile. It had a ladder back and a rush bottom. "Such a good chair," Mrs. Fish said, wiping her face. "Should we save it, Joycie?"

I carried it over to Old Dad. "Can this be fixed?"

"Might be," he said, fingering it with his good hand.
"I'd fix it if I had both my hands. I've fixed lots of things.
Stoves, fridges, TVs, washers, dryers, tables and chairs,
and even a few Coke coolers. And everything I fix, somebody wants."

"People will pay for good old things," Mrs. Fish said.

"The money don't matter," Old Dad said.

"True. It's not the money. It's the satisfaction."

They were actually talking to each other. Now if only
Old Dad would say something nice to Mrs. Fish. Tell her
thank you for coming. And say she'd been a big help. But
instead, when she got in her car and raced the motor, he
yelled at her. "Take it easy! Cowboy! Where do you think
you're going!"

"Down to the gate, Mr. Adams." Mrs. Fish waved out
the window. "Drive down with me, Joycie, and you can
lock up."

As soon as I was in the car, she said, "Joycie, I don't
mean to pry, but does your Old Dad have money for
food?"

I nodded. "He gets his paycheck, Mrs. Fish."

"Then why don't you have anything in your icebox or
on your shelves? I peeked when I went to the little girls'
room."

"Old Dad can't drive now," I said. "So we can't shop."

"I should have thought!" Mrs. Fish said. "Dear one, I'll
take you shopping tomorrow right after school. Do you
have enough food till then?"

"Yes, thank you, Mrs. Fish." I touched her hand. "Mrs.
Fish. You're good," I said, feeling shy.

The next day after school we went shopping, so I didn't
work in the dump, but the other days I did.

Over the weekend Mrs. Fish came and we got every-

thing fixed up right again. Then the next week it got
worse again, smelly, junky, and awful. Old Dad was
gloomy. He held his bad hand by the wrist and shook it,
ordering it to move. "Stupid hand! Move, or I'll chop you
off and throw you away with the rest of the garbage."

"You're getting better, Old Dad," I said. I really did
think his leg was a little better, not dragging so much.

"Tell that to your fancy friend," he said. "You don't
have to lie to me."

"Mrs. Fish isn't fancy!" Sometimes I felt so bad for him;
sometimes I just felt mad at him. He still didn't act very
nice to Mrs. Fish. And she did everything for us.

That Friday she took me shopping again. If it weren't
for Mrs. Fish we wouldn't even have had food in the
house. And Old Dad knew it.

On the way back to the house, Mrs. Fish asked me what
Old Dad and I were going to have for supper. I said some
of the ham we'd bought. "It'll be so good, Mrs. Fish."

"Ham is my favorite, too. By the way, dear one, you
don't have to call me Mrs. Fish all the time. Emily would
do nicely."

"Oh! But Mrs. Fish sounds better. I mean, it's more re-
spectful."

"What's your Old Dad's first name?" Mrs. Fish said,
zooming past a car.

"Henry," I said.

"Henry. Henry Adams. What a very good name." She
smiled over at me.

At the dump we stopped for Old Dad. Mrs. Fish helped
him into the car. "Don't shove me, Fish!"

"Now, now, dear man, I'm not shoving you."

We drove to the house. Mrs. Fish pointed to Face Pole.
"I've been dying to know. What *is* that?"

"Face Pole," I said. "Old Dad carves on it."

Mrs. Fish got out of the car and walked around Face Pole. "My," she said. "My, my! That is impressive." She stood up on her toes, then walked around it again. "I am impressed!" she said again. Her hands were linked behind her back, and she nodded like a judge. "Some people have *talent!*"

We carried in the groceries. Mrs. Fish put down the last bag. "I'd stay for supper . . . if someone invited me," she sang out. She looked at Old Dad. He just grunted.

"I'll invite you, Mrs. Fish!" I said. "You're invited!"

"Why, thank you, dear one," she said, sounding as happy as if I had thought of it myself. "You and I will make supper together."

We made the ham and baked potatoes and egg custard for dessert. Delicious smells filled the house. I set the table with three bowls, forks and spoons. "Napkins?" Mrs. Fish said.

My face got red. I'd forgotten to buy them. "Never you mind," Mrs. Fish said. "I always forget something. Do you have any candles, Joycie?" I climbed up on a chair and took down our jar of emergency candles from a high shelf. Mrs. Fish lit two, dripped wax into saucers and set the candles in the middle of the table.

When the food was ready she shut off all the lights. "What's going on?" Old Dad said.

"We're eating by candlelight, Henry."

"I like to see what I eat," Old Dad said. "Joyce, turn on the lights."

I turned on one light. "I'm sorry, Mrs. Fish."

"Perfectly all right," she said. "The food will taste just as good."

I didn't think the food could taste any better. "It's wonderful," I said. "Better than anything I ever make."

"And how are you enjoying the meal, Henry?" she said.

Old Dad tapped his fingers on the table. "It's okay," he said.

I stared at his fingers. "Old Dad." I almost choked on the spoonful of custard in my mouth. "Old Dad . . . your fingers . . . your *hand* . . ." I was so excited my spoon went flying out of my hand. "Your hand, Old Dad! Your bad hand—you're tapping!"

It was true. He was tapping the table with his dead fingers.

"My fingers . . . my fingers," Old Dad said. "My fingers . . ." I started to cry. Old Dad tapped his fingers, tapped and tapped. He kept tapping his fingers, and looking at them, and laughing.

16

Mrs. Fish Sleeps Over

Looking out the window of my room, I saw a deer step out of the woods. "Hello," I said. There was a light sprinkling of snow on the ground. The deer lifted one front foot, then turned and was gone in a breath.

"It snowed, Old Dad," I called.

"Won't last long," he said.

He was right. By the time I met Mrs. Fish at the gate, the sun had melted all the snow.

"And how is the dear man on this fine Saturday morning?"

"Frisky," I said. "He's already working."

"Since his fingers started moving, he's cheered right up. Two weeks has made all the difference!"

When we got to the dump she said, "Good morning, Henry. What are we doing today?" She pulled on her big gray work gloves. "Our usual good works?"

Old Dad tipped his cap over his eyes. "Fish, you don't have to do anything."

Mrs. Fish looked around. "I don't understand. There's

plenty of work." Old Dad still couldn't keep up with the garbage that came in every day.

"I appreciate all what you've done," Old Dad said. "but we don't need you no more."

"Yes we do, Old Dad," I said.

"Quiet, Joyce!" He started dragging a broken old couch to the edge of the ravine. The legs dragged in the sand. Old Dad was having a lot of trouble. Without saying a word, Mrs. Fish picked up the other end and together they heaved it over the side.

"See, Old Dad!" I said. He thought he was better, but he was still not as strong as he was before. He didn't have that much use of his left hand, and he was slow on his feet. And his face was still different. Everything on the left side—eye, nose, mouth—was lower than everything on the right side.

He put on his stubborn look. "Fish has done enough This ain't her place."

"It's my pleasure," Mrs. Fish said.

"Some pleasure. Handling garbage."

"Oh, garbage," she said, waving her hand. "I don't call it garbage. I call it . . . gar-*baaj*! I call it . . . sanitary engineering!"

That made old Dad smile. He didn't say anything else about us not needing Mrs. Fish. Later in the day I asked her if she'd stay to supper with us.

Mrs. Fish looked at Old Dad. "If it's all right with everybody." He didn't say yes, but he didn't say no, either.

"Tell her to stay, Old Dad."

"Don't ask me. It's up to her."

"It's all right with me," Mrs. Fish said, winking at me.

"And it's all right with me," I said. "So you're staying."

Mrs. Fish and I made supper while Old Dad took a nap.

He'd taken a long nap after lunch, too. We made Hungarian goulash and corn bread. While it was cooking, Mrs. Fish cut grapefruits and put maraschino cherries in the middle of each half. She put the grapefruit on a little plate, and the little plate on a bigger plate. Then she showed me how to set the table. Napkins folded on the left side, forks on napkins, and knives and spoons on the right side of the plate.

"And the water glass here," she said, putting a glass above each knife. "Now light the candles, Joyce, and we're all ready." She tapped a spoon against a glass. "Supper," she called.

Old Dad came slowly into the kitchen, leaning on his stick. He was stiff from sleeping. "What's that?" he said, pointing to the grapefruits. "I never saw grapefruit for supper."

"It's an appetizer, dear man."

We sat down. The room was dim in the candlelight. The fire in the stove made flickering shadows on the wall. Even though he grumbled, Old Dad ate the grapefruit. He ate a steaming plateful of goulash, and buttered corn bread, and asked for seconds on everything.

"Will you ask me my spelling words after supper, Old Dad?" I said. "I got three wrong on our test Friday."

"You don't take after me then," he said. "I was spelling champion in my school."

"You never told me that."

He looked at Mrs. Fish from the corner of his eye. "I was the best speller in sixth grade. Seventh grade, too."

"Then what happened?" Mrs. Fish said.

"Left school."

"Too early," Mrs. Fish said. "I left school early, too. I was just a slip of a lass. I've always been sorry. I thirst for knowledge."

"Left school when I was thirteen," Old Dad said. "Never went back. My father didn't care. He wanted me to go to work. Life was hard in those days. He wanted me to be as hard as life."

"Life is never easy," Mrs. Fish said.

I sat back. I didn't want to make a sound. Old Dad and Mrs. Fish were talking. Really talking to each other.

"I ain't complaining," Old Dad said.

"You've got Joycie," Mrs. Fish said. "That's a blessing."

"Right," Old Dad said. He sat back and worked the fingers of his bad hand. "Everything ain't so good, though. Crippled . . . being a cripple . . ."

"You're getting better every day, dear man!"

Old Dad's mouth slipped down. "*Dear man.* I ain't no one's dear man."

"Oh, that's just my way. You'd rather I called you Henry?"

"Call me anything. Call me what everyone calls me. I told you—call me Ape."

"Dear ma—— Henry! I don't like names like that."

Old Dad made his ape face. "Why not? It's me, ain't it?"

"What we look like is only a little part of the story, it's only the outside of the package. The real you is like a light shining through."

Old Dad laughed silently. "A flashlight!"

"A bright beam of light!" Mrs. Fish said.

"My light ain't so bright these days."

"Oh, I know," Mrs. Fish said. "There are good times in life and bad times. I've had my share of both. After Mama died I thought I'd never be happy again. There never was a sadder person in the world than me. So many years I spent running . . . and looking . . . moving here and there . . . city to city . . . job to job . . . looking, always looking." Her eyes were wet. "But now I have William and Greta, Toot Sweet, my cozy room, and"—she reached out for my hand—"my friends. I have Joycie, and I have you. What else is life all about?"

We were all quiet for a moment. I had that queer feeling of being sad and happy at the same time. Then Old Dad pushed back his chair. "Yup! Enough talk."

"Yup!" Mrs. Fish echoed. "Time for dancing." She grabbed Old Dad and danced him slowly around the room.

"Hey! Hey," he cried. "Let go of me."

"Dance, Old Dad," I said. "Go on!" His foot dragged, his arm hung by his side.

"You're doing beautifully, dear man!"

"Okay, okay." He fell into a chair. "Fish, you're too much," he said, but he was smiling.

After we cleaned up, Mrs. Fish said it was time for her to go. "My babies will be wondering where I am." She put on her coat and scarf and got her big pocketbook with the wooden handles. "Well, I'm off. Toodle-oo, Henry."

I walked with her down to the dump where she'd left her car. There was a big red moon coming up in the east. It was quiet. Nights like these I just wanted to breathe quietly.

Mrs. Fish slid into her car and closed the door. "Good-bye, again." She turned on the ignition. Nothing happened. She tried it again. "My battery's dead," she said. "Of all the silly things—"

"You can stay overnight with us," I said happily.

"But, dear one, I don't think there's room for me."

"Yes there is, Mrs. Fish. Upstairs in my room. You sleep in my bed, and I'll sleep on the floor. I don't mind!"

She tried the car again. It was still dead. "In the morning Old Dad can look at it," I said. "He'll fix it. Please stay, Mrs. Fish. Nobody ever stayed before."

"Nobody?" she said.

"No," I said. "You'd be the first one."

She put her arm around me. "I'm honored."

In my room I made a bed on the floor. I took Mama Big Joyce Doll and got under the blankets. Under her overalls Mrs. Fish wore enormous bloomers with rubber around the legs. Her breasts were big and soft and white. She got into bed and pulled the blankets over herself. "This is cozy. Are you comfortable, Joycie? Maybe I should change with you—"

"No, I'm fine," I said. It was a little bit hard, but I didn't care. "Will William and Greta be all right, Mrs. Fish?"

"Oh, yes. I left them lots of food and water this morning. Well, nighty-night. Sleep tight."

I closed my eyes. After a while I whispered, "Mrs. Fish? Are you sleeping?"

"Mmm, not yet, dear. What is it?"

"What happened to your husband?"

"Never had one," she said sleepily. "They just started calling me Mrs., so I let them."

She fell asleep first. I listened to her breathing. It made me think of something long, long ago . . . so long ago it was when I was living with my mother. I was in a crib . . . next to me someone was sleeping, breathing evenly. I remembered feeling happy.

In the morning we ate breakfast all together. Mrs. Fish made poached eggs, Old Dad made toast, and I made cereal. "People should stoke up in the morning," Mrs. Fish said.

Old Dad held out his coffee cup for a refill. "Good coffee, Fish."

We ate, then cleaned up. Mrs. Fish talked and joked. She said she was a morning person. "What about you, Henry?"

"Morning, night, I'm the same," he said.

At the dump Mrs. Fish took the battery out of her car and put it into LT, so we could take it to town and get it charged.

"You know, Henry, you don't have to come," Mrs. Fish said, getting behind the wheel. "I can take care of it."

"I'm gonna keep an eye on my truck."

"Oh, you don't like the way I drive. Sit next to me, Joycie. We'll let Henry sit next to the door for a quick getaway." She drove fast down our road, just to tease him.

"Slow down! You drive like a darn cowboy."

"I'm an old cow*hand*," Mrs. Fish sang. "Come on, sing with me. Joyce. Henry." I started to sing. "I'm an old cow*hand*, on the Rio *Grande*. . . ." And though we couldn't get Old Dad to sing along, he had his right hand out the window, beating on the door in time to our singing.

After that, when Mrs. Fish came to help on Saturdays, she stayed overnight, and worked with us again on Sunday. She said staying over made a lot of sense. It saved her two trips. Saturdays after we finished work she'd take her little striped suitcase upstairs, and change into a dress. She had one patterned with gold and brown leaves that came down to her ankles which was my favorite. She'd put on necklaces and bracelets, comb her hair and put in her enameled butterfly barrettes. "Mama gave me these," she said. "They're very special."

I'd change, too, then we'd go downstairs and cook supper. Sometimes Mrs. Fish and I would do everything and let Old Dad rest. But sometimes the three of us would cook together. Those were the best times. After supper we talked or played cards. One night Mrs. Fish and I played Spit, slapping down our cards hard and yelling out, "Spit!"

"What a stupid game," Old Dad said, but he wanted to play too.

Later, Mrs. Fish went up with me to help fix my bed on the floor. "Don't forget your baby," she said, smoothing down Mama Big Joyce Doll's yellow yarn braids.

"Do you think it's silly for me to sleep with Mama Big Joyce Doll, Mrs. Fish? Because I'm so old, I mean?"

"My, no. You love her, and that's what counts." She bent over me, tucking in the covers. She patted my arm. "Good night, dear one. I'll stay up and talk to Henry for a bit."

Downstairs, I heard her high voice, then Old Dad's rumbly voice, then her high voice again. It was like singing. I wriggled around, getting comfortable. Listening to Mrs. Fish and Old Dad talking was so cozy. Even better than having Mrs. Fish sleeping in my room.

I dreamed about them. They were in the brass bed together. The covers were up to their chins. Only their heads showed. Mrs. Fish was talking, and Old Dad was listening. Then I came down and we all ate breakfast. We had blue mugs. Our names were on them. OLD DAD. MRS. FISH. JOYCE. And I thought, Now we are a family.

Then Mrs. Fish was in my room. I saw her shadow, big and dark, moving around. Was I still dreaming? She bent over me. I smelled toothpaste and soap. Swiftly, like a bird flying into a nest, she darted down and kissed me. "Dear one," she said. "Dear one." I wanted to say thank you, and tell her about my dream. But then I really was asleep again.

❦ 17 ❧

The Lost Barrette

"Where do you think the Fish is?" Old Dad said. It was Saturday, and Mrs. Fish hadn't been at the gate in the morning. Now it was nearly noon and she still hadn't come. "Think she got tired of us?"

"Not Mrs. Fish," I said.

"Eh, that's the way people are," he said.

"Maybe she's sick."

"Sick?" Old Dad shook his head. "Not her. Not that big fine-looking woman."

"Anybody can get sick, Old Dad. You did."

He leaned on the rake. "You think Fish is lying on the ground somewhere, like me?"

"Don't say that! You scare me."

"You get scared too easy, Joyce. I'll tell you why Fish ain't here. Two plain reasons. One. She got tired of working in the dump. Two. She got tired of seeing the Ape."

"That's wrong," I said. "And it's dumb besides."

He swung his head around. "Now don't start sassing me, Joyce."

110

"Okay! I'm sorry! But Mrs. Fish likes coming here, Old Dad. We're company. She likes us."

"Likes you."

"Likes you, too!"

"Huh! Tell me another." He slowly raked the drop-off apron smooth. "Let's get some work done here."

When it was time to lock up, Old Dad climbed into LT. "Get in." He was behind the wheel.

"What're we going to do? You can't drive."

"Watch me!" He turned on the key with his right hand. That was okay. He pushed in the clutch with his right foot. But after that he had trouble. He couldn't hold the wheel and handle the shift with one hand. "I'll clutch, and you shift," he said. So that's the way we drove.

I thought we were only going to the gate, but Old Dad drove right through. He stopped for me to lock the gate. "Where are we going?" I said when I got back in the truck.

"First gear. Let's go. Let's get there, then you'll see."

We drove into town with me shifting and Old Dad doing the rest. It worked okay, even if it wasn't very smooth.

On Market Street where Mrs. Fish lived, Old Dad parked the truck. I still didn't catch on. I thought we were going shopping. Then he said, "Go see if the Fish is okay."

"Old Dad!" I hugged him. "You're wonderful."

"Why're you always hugging me and kissing me?" he said, wiping his mouth.

"Because I love you."

"That's all right," he said. "But you gotta watch it. Don't go around kissing everyone."

"Just you, Old Dad."

"Don't be funny, Joyce. Get going now. See what's the matter with Fish."

"I'll tell her you want to know," I said, opening the truck door.

"Hey! It was your idea."

"Two great minds on the same track. Why don't you come up too?"

He shook his head. He looked tired. He was thin from being sick, and I could see all the bones in his face.

I ran up the stairs and knocked on Mrs. Fish's door. Greta started barking. Mrs. Fish opened the door. She was wearing a long pink nightgown. "Joyce," she whispered. "How nice. Come in, dear one. I've lost my voice. Bad cold. Don't come close."

"Are you all right? We missed you today."

"I'll be right as rain in another couple days," she whispered. "How'd you get here?"

"Old Dad and I drove, Mrs. Fish. He steered and I shifted."

"What a way to drive," she whispered.

"Old Dad was worried about you, Mrs. Fish."

"Why, the dear man." She went to the window and waved. Old Dad flapped his hand, and Mrs. Fish blew him a kiss. "Tell him I've just got a little cold, Joyce. Nothing serious. I'll be back at the dump next week."

She was out of school most of the week. I missed her and could hardly wait for Saturday.

But on Saturday something terrible happened. It was noontime. We were all sitting on the bench in the sun eating our lunches. "Not many more of these beautiful days left, I'm afraid," Mrs. Fish said. She was still sniffling, but much better. "I smell winter creeping into the air. How do you work here in winter, Henry?"

"Same as now," he said. "Hard."

"Oh, I look forward to winter. I like being out in the cold. It freshens up the blood."

Old Dad slapped his lazy left arm. "You won't be freshening up here, Fish."

"Why, surely I will," Mrs. Fish said. "Just so long as you need me, I'll be here."

"Well," Old Dad said, "I don't need you. You done enough. You done plenty. I thank you, but I can handle things okay from now on."

"Old Dad!" I poked him. "What are you saying?"

"Butt out, Joyce. I've been thinking about it. We've taken enough from Fish. The dump's no place for a woman like her. Garbage dump . . . uh-uh. I don't want her to come here anymore."

I grabbed his hand. "Mrs. Fish likes it here. Don't you, Mrs. Fish?" She wasn't saying anything. "We need her." My head swung back and forth between them. "We need you, Mrs. Fish. Don't listen to Old Dad."

"Hey, Joyce! I just said something. We can handle this dump now. You and me together, the way it's always been."

"I don't want you to send Mrs. Fish away," I cried.

"It ain't right for her," he said. "Fish knows it, don't you, Fish?"

"Oh, I know you'll do fine without me," Mrs. Fish said. "This is really wonderful, Joyce. Such a wonderful recovery." She was smiling and winking and beaming, but I couldn't smile back. "Do you want me to work the rest of the day, Henry?"

"No need," he said.

"All right, then, as you say. I'll be going now." She closed her lunch box.

"When will I see you, Mrs. Fish?"

"Why, we'll see each other in school, dear one." She hugged me hard. Her eyes were shiny. "We'll visit. We can't let things go." She put her hand to her hair. "Oh, dear, oh, dear. I lost my butterfly barrette. Yesterday I was looking for it and couldn't find it. I knew it was a bad sign. I don't know when I lost it, or where. Will you look around the house for it, Joyce?"

"Your beautiful barrette," I said. My throat was tight.

Mrs. Fish got into her car. She stuck her big shaggy head out the window. "I'll be saying good-bye, Henry."

"Yeah. Well. Good-bye, then," Old Dad said. He thumped his stick, looked like he was going to say something else, then went into the work shack.

"Joycie. Kiss kiss."

I leaned toward her. "Kiss kiss." I felt her black whiskers brush against my cheek.

"There," she said. Her eyes were wet. "Don't feel bad. We'll see each other, dear child." She drove away.

After that the whole day was terrible. People were rude, I cut my finger on some metal, and Old Dad yelled at me for everything. Supper was even worse. We didn't make anything special, and we hardly talked.

After supper Old Dad tried to thread a needle to sew up a rip in his jacket, but his left hand shook so he kept missing the eye. I took the needle and thread from him. He tried to take it back. "I can do it okay!"

"Stubborn," I said furiously, darting away from him. "You think you can do *everything* yourself!"

"I told you, Joyce! This ain't her place. Give me that needle."

"You just wait!" I held the needle up and threaded it away from him. "You'll be sorry, Old Dad. All the times she helped us—" I threw the threaded needle down on the table. "Here! Go ahead, sew your jacket! Don't ask me to help!"

"Sassy," he said. "Sass! That's what you learned from her." He punched the needle into his jacket sleeve.

"Oh, no," I said, "No, no, you know that's not true. You hurt Mrs. Fish's feelings, but she was too polite to say anything. She's always nice. She has wonderful manners."

"What's she got to be hurt about? I did her a favor."

"Mrs. Fish—"

"Fish, Fish . . . that all you can say?"

"You like her, too," I said. "Don't pretend!"

"Listen!" Old Dad bit off the thread and stuck the needle in the spool. "It's got nothing to do with liking. Didn't I teach you anything? Didn't I tell you all the time about being independent? What'd I tell you, Joyce? *You don't depend on nobody. You depend on yourself.* Otherwise, you're in for grief. Nothing but grief."

"How about when you got sick?" I said. "You needed me. You needed Mrs. Fish."

"What do you know? That was only temporary. I could have hired somebody to work here temporary." He hung the jacket on a peg. "Don't you tell me I needed. I don't need nobody."

"Maybe you don't even need me." I was smiling. It was stupid to smile. But I couldn't stop, and all the time I was smiling, I felt terrible. "Maybe you want to throw me out, too," I said. "Like garbage. The way you threw out Mrs. Fish."

"Hey! Is that a nice way to talk to your Old Dad? You think that's the way I feel about you? You think I don't have feelings?"

Tears came to my eyes. I rushed to him and hugged him. "I'm sorry, Old Dad. I'm sorry."

"Okay. Okay," he said. He put his hand on my head. "Okay, we're both feeling a little bad tonight. But you listen to me, Joyce. I'm doing what's right You start depending on people, you just got misery ahead. Now I know that for a fact."

"Okay," I whispered. I went upstairs and got in bed, cuddling Mama Big Joyce Doll. Downstairs I heard Old Dad shuffling restlessly around. *Booom* . . *shuush* . . *booom* . . . *shuush*. . . . Good foot stamped, bad foot dragged. *Booom* . *shuush* . . *booom*   *shuush*

18

A Fish, and An Ape, and A Crazy Girl

"Mrs. Fish, will you come to visit us Saturday?" I was in her room at lunch.

"You're going to be working Saturday, Joycie. I'll just be in the way."

"After work, Mrs. Fish. You could come for supper and stay over."

Mrs. Fish fussed with William's collar. "Oh, your Old Dad doesn't want me bothering him, Joyce."

"No, Mrs. Fish, he wants you to come too."

She picked up William and held him under her chin. "Did he say so, Joyce?"

I shook my head. "No, but he does want you, Mrs. Fish. I know he does."

"Well, we'll see," she said, stroking William. "We-eee'll see!"

All day Saturday I made deals with myself. *If I get that wood stacked in twenty minutes, Mrs. Fish will come when we're done working. If five green cars drive in to the dump . . . If I give half my lunch to the birds . . .*

And later, walking down the road to lock up the gate, I kept on hoping. I didn't run. I walked as slowly as I could . . . to give her time to come. I stopped to watch a flock of blackbirds rising out of a tree, then settling in again. I picked some dried goldenrod for the house. I saw the evening star, closed my eyes, and wished. *Please come see us, Mrs. Fish.*

At the gate I looked both ways down the road, checked our mailbox, and then closed the gate slowly and put on the lock. I looked down the road again. A car was coming. My heart began beating wildly. I jumped up on the gate, waving. "Mrs. Fish!" The car sped by.

Then I knew she wasn't coming. I left the goldenrod lying in the road near the gate. I didn't want flowers in the house. My eyes stung, but I wouldn't let myself cry. *Don't be a nit, Joyce. You'll see her Monday.*

At lunchtime Monday I went straight down to the basement and knocked on Mrs. Fish's door. A very thin man opened it. I knew him from somewhere. "Yeah?" he said. It was Charlie, our school's last-year's custodian.

"Where's Mrs. Fish?" I said.

"What?" He fingered his hearing aid.

"Mrs. Fish. *Mrs. Fish.*"

"Who's that?"

"The custodian!" I said.

"I'm the custodian."

"Where's Mrs. Fish?" My hands were wet.

"Fish?" he said. "Why don't you go upstairs?"

I looked past him. No animal pictures on the walls, no yellow and red flowers on the table. No William. *No Mrs. Fish.* I got so scared I could hardly breathe. I had the crazy thought that maybe Mrs. Fish was someone I dreamed, not real at all.

"What are you doing here?" I said.

"I'm the custodian. I'm Charlie. I had an operation, been on leave. I just came back today. What do you want? Your teacher want something?"

I backed away, shaking my head. I went into the girls' room and sat down in one of the booths until it was time to go back to my room.

That night I told Old Dad about Charlie, and that Mrs. Fish was gone. "That's what they do to you," he said. "They don't need you, they throw you out. How come the Fish didn't tell us?"

"I don't know," I choked. "We have to go see her."

"Hey! Don't worry. If I know Fish she's got another job already."

I wasn't worried about that. It was not seeing Mrs. Fish at all that was so terrible. I missed her. Friday, when we went into town, I could hardly eat my supper. "Hurry up, Old Dad!"

"Eat your fries."

"I don't want them."

"I'll eat them," he said. And I had to wait while he did.

Finally we were on Market Street. I ran up the stairs and knocked on Mrs. Fish's door. Greta barked. "Mrs. Fish," I called, "it's me!" But there was no reply. A door down the hall opened.

"Hello there, you looking for Emily?"

"Yes. I'm a friend."

"She's working, honey." Mrs. Fish's neighbor was wearing jeans and a plaid shirt. She had a book in her hand. "Want me to tell her you were here?"

"Do you know where she's working?"

"Sure do, honey. First Methodist over on Elm Street. She comes home about nine, ten usually."

I bit my lip. We'd be back at the dump by then. "Will you tell her Joyce was here, and ask her to come visit us on Sunday?"

"Sure will, honey. But I can tell you right now she won't come. She works all weekend. Those are her busiest days."

The week after that was the worst of my life. I didn't think I'd ever see Mrs. Fish again. I was really depressed. I didn't want to go to school. I had nowhere to go for lunch, no one to talk to. One day I was walking in the hall when Linda Justice and Sharon Mason saw me. They spread out so I couldn't get past them. "Look who's here," Linda said.

"The Dump Queen," Sharon said.

"The Smelly Queen," Linda said.

They fanned their noses. "Help! I'm going to faint from the smell."

"Move," I said. I was ready to fight. I didn't care if they threw me out of school forever. "Get out of my way, or I'll punch you out."

"I'm really scared," Sharon said, but she moved aside.

Every day I thought about Mrs. Fish. I was lonely. Saturday night was the worst. I kept remembering when Mrs. Fish was with us—how good the food was, how pretty the table looked, how much fun we had. Old Dad was laughing then!

I just couldn't stand it. "Old Dad!" I threw my arms around him. "I miss her! I miss Mrs. Fish."

"You think you're the only—" He broke off.

"What?" I said.

"Nothing." He pulled my hands away and stomped into the living room. I ran after him.

"What were you going to say? You started to say about Mrs. Fish."

"I didn't start to say nothing."

"Yes, you did."

"Hey! I didn't say nothing."

"Old Dad, you were going to say, 'You think you're the only one who misses her!' "

"Don't talk crazy. Go make supper. I'm going for wood."

I put soup bowls on the table and crackers and the jar of apple butter. I kept thinking, *He misses her, too!* Why should we miss Mrs. Fish, and why should she miss us, and not all three of us be together? It would make sense to live together.

I began to dream about it. We'd eat supper together every night. We'd have candles on the table, Mrs. Fish's plastic flowers, and she'd call us with a little bell. In the morning she'd make good coffee while Old Dad made the breakfast, and I fixed our lunches. We'd all be happy. I couldn't understand why I hadn't thought of it sooner.

As soon as Old Dad came back with the wood, I told him my idea.

"Old Dad, I want Mrs. Fish to come live with us."

"Fish come *here*?" He looked startled. "She wouldn't do that. Who said it?"

"I'm saying it. It's my own idea. I bet she'd come if you asked her."

"Well, I ain't asking." He shoved wood into the stove. "What do we need somebody else for? We get along just fine. And nobody tells us what to do."

"Old Dad, it would be easy to ask," I said. "You just say, 'Emily, I miss you. I think it would be nice if you came to live with Joyce and me.' "

He banged down the stove lid. "You need sense talked into you! How many times do I have to tell you—I don't ask no one for nothin'!"

"Why do you have to be so stubborn?" I cried. "What's so terrible about asking for something?"

"Don't be stupid. This ain't just *something*."

"That's right!" I said fiercely. "This is *important*. It's too important for you to be stubborn."

"It ain't never been anyone but us—"

"*First*, it was just you," I interrupted. "Then it was you and me. Now it could be you, me, and Mrs. Fish."

He squinched his eyes at me and mumbled under his breath.

I poured soup into our bowls and sat down, but I couldn't eat. "Wouldn't you just try?" I pleaded. "See what she says? It couldn't hurt anything."

"Eat." He pushed the bread toward me.

"I'm not hungry." I choked up.

"Are you going to cry?" he said. "I'm trying to eat."

I shook my head.

"Don't you cry."

"I won't, I won't." A tear leaked down my cheek.

"You're crying!"

"No, I'm not!"

He picked up his soup bowl and drank his soup. I sank down in my seat. He was going into one of his no-talking moods. It was no use saying anything when he was that way. He drank two cups of coffee. I didn't say anything, either.

"Joyce—" He pushed away his coffee cup. "Hell's bells! What do you want me to do? Go like a goddamn fool to the Fish? She'll laugh in my face."

"No, she won't!"

"Okay! She'll laugh behind my back. That what you want?"

"You know Mrs. Fish wouldn't do that. She likes you. She thinks you're wonderful."

"Crazy," he said. "You want me to do crazy things."

"No, I just want us all to be together, like . . . like a family."

"Some family. A fish, and an ape, and a crazy girl! And even if she did come here—" he said. "I'm just saying *if*, where would we put her? We don't have room for her."

I put my hands around my soup bowl. I was shivering. Was he going to do it? "There's plenty of room," I said, trying to sound calm. "She could sleep upstairs with me. Or down here with you."

"I can't ask her." He kept tearing the bread into little pieces. "No! Just can't. I don't know how to do things like that." He bent forward, showing me his hands. "What am I going to say to her? I don't know how."

We both sat there for a long time. I felt sadder and sadder. I felt sorry for me, and sorrier for Old Dad. I was sure he wanted Mrs. Fish to come live with us, just as much as I did. But he was afraid to ask.

"What if she knew you wanted her to come here," I said, "and you didn't even have to ask—"

"How's that going to happen?"

"I'm just saying, *What if*, Old Dad."

"I don't know," he said, shifting around in his seat. His eyes were very blue. "It might be okay."

"And," I continued, "Mrs. Fish would say, 'Yes, I'll come live with Joyce and Old Dad.'" I pushed away from the table and flung my arms around his neck. "Then it would all be settled!"

"That's a pretty story," he said, "but who's going to do the asking? Hey, you're choking me."

"I could ask," I blurted. "You want me to? I'll do it!"

He pulled my arms off his neck. "Suit yourself," he said. "She won't come. But you want to ask, go ahead. It's okay with me. See what she says, Joyce."

19

The Million-Dollar Question

I followed Mrs. Fish into her apartment. She was wearing a pink kimono with big blue and orange flowers, and an orange sash. She had on wooden clogs, and her toenails were painted orange. "I just had to see you, Mrs. Fish." I'd skipped school. First time I ever did it.

Greta frisked around my legs. "See how happy she is to see you," Mrs. Fish said. "And me—oh, I've missed you so!" She put her arms around me. I hugged her back. I didn't want to let her go. Greta barked, little shrill yaps that sounded like she was saying, "Hug me, too . . . hug me, toooo!"

Mrs. Fish smelled good . . . lemons and soap. "Oh, Mrs. Fish . . ."

"Dear one. I know, I know." She drew me into the room. "Come and sit down. Let me look at you. Oh, how pretty you are, my little Joycie!" We hugged again, then sat holding hands.

"How's your new job?" I said. "Do you like it?"

"Oh, it's just fine. But . . . I'm lonely at lunchtime. But, there, it's a job, isn't it. That's what counts."

"I went down to see you," I said. "And Charlie was there."

Mrs. Fish shook her head, her lips pursing. "Imagine, they told me that Monday morning. 'We just hired you till he comes back,' they said. 'You knew that. And now he's back.' Just like that. It was hardly decent. But never mind me. Tell me about you. How is everything? How's school?"

"It's awful," I said. "I hate it now that you're not there."

"I'm so sorry to hear you speak that way, Joyce. School is important." She picked up William and kissed his nose. "Isn't school important, William? You should learn everything you can, Joyce. It's a golden opportunity."

"You sound like Old Dad."

"Surely I do. We both came through the school of hard knocks."

In his cage, Toot Sweet hopped from bar to bar. Mrs. Fish fluttered her fingers at him. "Joyce, did you ever find my butterfly barrette?"

I shook my head. "I looked everywhere in my room, and downstairs. I'm sorry."

"Oh, dear," she said, "and I've looked everywhere here. Well, Mama always said, Don't cry over spilled milk, but all the same, I'll never find another barrette like that. And it was Mama's gift." She sighed. "Tell me, Joycie, how is the dear man getting on?"

"Good, Mrs. Fish, really good. His leg is still lazy, but he does almost everything."

"So glad, so glad. That was an unusual experience working in the dump with you and Henry. I enjoyed it."

"Mrs. Fish . . ." I looked around. Greta was standing with her paws on the windowsill looking out between the frame of green leaves and vines. Everything was so perfect and cozy in Mrs. Fish's apartment. Why would she want to leave all this, and come live with me and Old Dad?

"Mrs. Fish . . . Mrs. Fish . . ." My mouth was dry. "We miss you," I blurted. "Me and Old Dad. That's why I came."

"Oh, how nice. I'd love to work with you again, dear one."

"No, Mrs. Fish, not work." I looked at her. "We want you to come live with us."

"*Live* with you?"

I licked my lips. "Mrs. Fish . . . can you? Will you?"

"Whose idea was this, Joyce? I think it was yours."

I smiled hopefully at her. "Well . . . it was. But Old Dad wants it too."

"He said that?"

"Yes. He said it's all right with him if you come." It didn't sound too good, but Mrs. Fish knew Old Dad. She'd know what he meant.

Mrs. Fish picked up an Elvis Presley cup from a side table. "Is that what he said? What, exactly, did he say, Joyce? How did all this come about?"

"Well . . . I said, 'I want Mrs. Fish to live with us.' And he said, 'It's okay with me.' "

"Very decent of him," she said. She was sitting up very straight, turning the Elvis cup round and round in her hand. "Did he send you with this . . . *invitation*?"

Her cheeks were puffed out. I had never seen her so upset. I bit my lip. "Well. Yes. . . ."

"So, Henry didn't think it was important enough to come himself." She stood up, crossing her arms, then strode across the room and back again. "Now listen carefully to me, Joyce." I had never seen her look so big, so splendid, and so angry.

"You tell Henry that I am a person. I am a *woman*. I am not some old piece of trash in his dump that he can treat any way he wants!"

"But Mrs. Fish—"

"I'm very upset," she rushed on, walking up and down, tightening the sash on her kimono. "Very upset. Very, very upset. Oh, yes, I'm terribly upset, I really am." Her voice got shaky. Suddenly she sat down on the couch and began to cry.

It was terrible to see her cry. It was my fault. I'd done everything wrong. Now I didn't know what to do.

"No, I won't be treated like this," Mrs. Fish said. "It's not fair, it just isn't, just because I'm a big fat ugly woman."

"No! No, Mrs. Fish! No, you're beautiful."

"Oh, I know," she said. "I know what I look like." She rubbed her hand over the whiskers on her chin. "Crazy Fish. I know what they call me. I know what people think. They think they can say anything to me."

"Please, Mrs. Fish, please, Old Dad isn't that way."

"Yes, Old Dad. Old Dad, too! He's a man, isn't he?"

"Mrs. Fish, Mrs. Fish . . ." I tried to put my arms around her. I was crying too.

Mrs. Fish wiped her eyes. "Oh, what a fool. Joyce, I'm sure you think I'm a perfect fool."

I shook my head. "I don't, I couldn't. I just . . . *love* you. And I hope . . . I want . . . Oh, Mrs. Fish, won't you come live with us?"

She patted my hand. "Joyce, if it was just you and me, I would do it in a moment. But there's someone else to consider. There's Henry."

"But he *said*—"

She put her finger to my lips. "I know what he said.

But that's not the way things are, Joyce love. It's like manners. Manners are a way of showing that you care for people. That you aren't just thinking about yourself. Now, listen, I'm going to say this the best way I know how. If Henry really wants me to come live with him and with you, then he has to ask me himself."

"He will," I said, quickly. "I'm sure he will." But I knew he wouldn't. That wasn't Old Dad's way.

"And before he asks me," Mrs. Fish went on, "he has to come visit me. And he has to tell me *why* he wants me to live with him."

"Oh!" It was John Alden and Priscilla. *Speak for yourself, John.* "You want Old Dad to court you," I said.

"Why, yes." Mrs. Fish blushed. "You might put it that way."

Old Dad courting? That meant presents. That meant saying nice things, sweet things, words like *dear* and *darling*. Old Dad wouldn't do it. He had never in his life even called me anything but Joyce.

"If he courted you, Mrs. Fish, *then* would you come live with us?"

"I might," she said. "And then again I might not. It would all depend. That's not all there is to it."

"I know," I said. "There's love."

"Yes," Mrs. Fish said. "That's the million-dollar question."

20

The Butterfly Barrette

Old Dad and I were sitting at the table after supper. He was reading, at least I thought he was. He kept looking at me over the top of his magazine, and muttering under his breath. I was supposed to be doing homework, but what I was really doing was thinking about Old Dad and Mrs. Fish. Thinking about Old Dad's courting her. Bringing her a present, telling her he loved her. He had to do those things if he wanted her to live with us, but the more I thought about it, the less it seemed like anything Old Dad would do.

He wet his finger and turned another page. "Hey! Joyce!"

I looked up. "What is it, Old Dad?"

"You go see the Fish today?" He turned another page without looking at me.

"Yes."

"That all you got to say?"

"Noooo."

He put down the magazine. "What do I got to do—pull it out of you word by word?"

I took a pecan from the bowl and cracked it. I knew I had to tell him. There was no way out of it. "Mrs. Fish said if you want her to live with us, you have to go see her. You should bring her a present, and you have to tell her you love her"—I was talking fast—"and *you* have to do it, not me!"

"Hey!" He kicked the table with his good foot. "I can't do them things."

"She says love is the million-dollar question, Old Dad."

"Love!" He stamped over to the other side of the room and took his jacket off the peg.

"What are you going to do, Old Dad?"

"I don't know, Joyce, I don't know. But whatever it is I'll do it. You just forget about it!" He went out of the house.

Later he came back, but he didn't say anything about Mrs. Fish, or what he'd do, and I was afraid to ask him. When I went up to bed I couldn't get to sleep for a long time. I heard Old Dad limping around downstairs, first his good leg, then *thunk* with his bad leg.

I told myself I tried. There was nothing else I could do. Old Dad would never court Mrs. Fish, not the way she wanted. So, she'd stay in her place, and we'd stay in our place, and we'd never live together. Tears came to my eyes. I held Mama Big Joyce Doll and whispered to her, but it wasn't the way it used to be. Even Mama Big Joyce Doll couldn't make me feel better.

The next day in school I was still thinking about Old Dad and Mrs. Fish. Two times Mr. LaSorta asked me questions and I didn't even hear him. At lunchtime he stopped me on the way out of the room. "Joyce, I want to talk to you. Okay to eat your lunch here?"

I nodded and sat down again. He waited till all the kids were gone, then he sat down at his desk with his lunch bag. "Let me see what I've got," he said, lifting out a sandwich. "Liverwurst. Good deal. You like liverwurst, Joyce?"

"I never tasted it," I said. I felt sort of shy.

"Really? You ought to try it. Joyce, this morning you seemed a little out of it." He bit into his sandwich. "Is there anything wrong? Anything I could help you with?"

"No . . . it's just—personal, I guess."

"You mean, something a man couldn't help with?"

I shook my head. "No, it's not that. It's something about Old Dad."

He pulled the top off a little can of tomato juice. "I hope it's not serious."

"It is . . . to me."

"Is he sick, Joyce?"

"No, Mr. LaSorta. It's about—" I broke off. From the way Old Dad had talked the night before, whatever happened or didn't happen was going to be up to him and Mrs. Fish. It didn't matter what I said. "I wish I could tell you, Mr. LaSorta, but I don't think I should."

"No, I wouldn't want you to break any promises or speak out of turn. I just want you to know, Joyce, that I'm always here to talk to. Or if I can help you in any way—"

I folded my wax paper carefully. "I'm sorry about not paying attention this morning."

"Well, it's unusual for you," he said. "Generally I can count on you. I guess teachers get lazy. They know the students they can depend on to answer all their foolish questions."

We both laughed. He was so nice! Now that Mrs. Fish was gone, he was the best thing about school.

Thursday night, right after supper, Old Dad said we were going into town.

"We never shop on Thursday," I said.

"We're going into town," he repeated. He pulled off his torn shirt. "Change your clothes," he ordered. He walked toward the bathroom with his clean shirt and pants. "We're going to see the Fish," he said over his shoulder, and he closed the bathroom door.

For a moment I just stood there, then I ran upstairs and changed as fast as I could. I ran back downstairs. Old Dad was still in the bathroom. I heard the water running. I looked around. Old Dad was going to do it! He was going to ask Mrs. Fish. What if she came back with us tonight? Our room was so messy! I put all the dishes in the sink, swept the floor, and shook out the blankets on Old Dad's bed. I straightened the pillow, fluffing it and turning it. Underneath I saw something glittery. It was Mrs. Fish's butterfly barrette.

"Old Dad—" I started. Then I just dropped the barrette into my pocket.

Old Dad had his shirt buttoned up wrong. I tried to help him, but he pushed my hand away and did it himself. "Let's go, let's go," he said, pulling on his jacket. His hair was slicked down. He looked really nice.

Outside he grabbed one end of Face Pole with his good hand. "Joyce, take the other end," he ordered.

"What are we doing?" I said.

"It's the present."

"What present?"

"The one I have to bring her," he yelled.

"*Face Pole?*"

"She liked it, didn't she?"

"Yes, but it's so big."

"You got any better ideas?"

I shook my head. Between us we got Face Pole into the back of the truck.

All the way into town Old Dad muttered to himself. I was afraid to say anything. On Market Street he parked the truck in front of Mrs. Fish's house and got right out. He put one end of Face Pole under his good arm, and I held the other end with both hands.

Up the stairs we went, then down the hall. "Fish!" Old Dad called. "Fish, we're here."

She opened the door. Old Dad and I marched in. We set Face Pole slantwise in a corner. It was taller than the ceiling.

"What *is* this?" Mrs. Fish said.

"That's for you, Fish." Old Dad wiped his hands down the side of his pants. "You like that present?" he asked Mrs. Fish.

She was laughing, moving around, her hands clasped in front of her. "I can't believe it. Did you really bring that for me?"

"It's the present," Old Dad said. "It's not finished, but it's pretty good."

"I thank you!" Mrs. Fish said. "What a magnificent gift. I've never had anything like this in my life."

William scampered up Face Pole, digging in his claws. "Hey! Down there!" Old Dad yelled.

"He thinks it's a giant scratching post," Mrs. Fish said.

"I didn't bring it for him," Old Dad said. He shuffled around the room. "What kind of room is this?" he said. "I never seen such a little place packed with so much stuff." He swung his arm, almost knocking a plaster angel off a table.

"These are all my things," Mrs. Fish said. "My possessions. My treasures. Each one has a special little memory for me."

Old Dad looked around the room, at the cups and bells and bowls, the plastic fruits, the china cats and stuffed animals. "You mean all this junk?"

"Don't call my things junk!"

"I don't like plastic."

"That is your privilege," Mrs. Fish said. "I happen to find a great many lovely things that are made of plastic." Her chin was up.

"You want to bring all that stuff with you?" he said. "You can't spread it around." He scratched his chin. "I guess I could give you a couple of shelves."

Mrs. Fish's eyes bulged. "What are you saying, Henry?"

Old Dad looked up at the ceiling. There were big sweat patches on his shirt. "You might as well come live with me and Joyce," he muttered.

Oh, no. He was doing it all wrong. *Tell her you like her. Tell her you love her. Just say—Fish, I love you.*

"Might—as—well—come—*live*—with—you?" Mrs. Fish repeated. Her cheeks had bright spots of color on them. She was getting upset. I could see it happening. She was getting very upset.

Old Dad edged toward the door. "You think about it, Fish. I brought you a present. I'll be going now. Come on, Joyce."

"Just a *minute*," Mrs. Fish said, "Think about *what*?"

"You know!" Old Dad had his hand on the doorknob.

"I only know what I hear," Mrs. Fish said, "and I haven't heard much."

"Well, I've said all I'm going to say." I recognized Old Dad's stubborn voice. I felt sick. First he'd insulted Mrs. Fish's pretty possessions, then he hadn't said anything right, and now he was just walking out. It was awful. My eyes filled. I dug my hands into my pockets. My fingers found the barrette.

"Mrs. Fish, I found your barrette." I handed it to her.

"Why, Joycie, thank you, dear. At least something good—" She bit her lip. "Where did you find it, dear one?"

"Under Old Dad's pillow," I said.

Old Dad's face turned red. He and Mrs. Fish looked at each other. "Why, Henry," Mrs. Fish said. "How very romantic."

Sweat burst out on Old Dad's face. "It wasn't nothing," he said. "I wasn't keeping it. I just picked it up."

"When was that?" Mrs. Fish said sweetly.

"Oh . . . oh . . . a while back."

"I understand," Mrs. Fish said. Now she was smiling. "You're a dear man. I always knew it." The ribbons on her blouse fluttered with her breathing. She kept looking at Old Dad. "Don't go yet. Is there something more you want to say?"

Old Dad looked up, then down. He shuffled his feet.

"Mrs. Fish . . . Emily . . . You see how it is. . . ." He sighed. "Well . . ." He stopped, cleared his throat. "Might as well be hung for a sheep as for a goat," he muttered. Then rushing on, he said, "I ain't much . . . just the Ape. . . . The ugly Ape Man. . . . My legs are bad, I got that lazy one, and this arm here, this left one, it ain't so much. I got feeling in my hand, but it's not one hundred percent. . . ."

He shook his head. "You probably don't want to come live with me. You're fine-looking . . . you've got manners . . . you know how to do things . . . you're too good for a dump . . . too good for Henry Adams."

"Dear Henry." Mrs. Fish took a step toward Old Dad

"Dear Henry . . . I don't know what to say. I esteem you. You're a good man, a great man, you have courage . . . you have heart. I love you and Joyce. But I must know—you still haven't said it—do you want me to come live with you? Do you love me?"

Old Dad looked past Mrs. Fish's shoulder. Everything seemed to go utterly still. William was sleeping. Greta lay with her face on her paws. I knew that I couldn't die standing there, but I thought that maybe I would if Old Dad didn't speak.

At last Old Dad nodded his head. "I do, Fish," he said, hoarsely. "Yes, I do."

21

Swiss Cheese Again!

On a Sunday at the end of November, Old Dad and I drove into town to help Mrs. Fish move. It was a perfect day. The sky was blue, and all along our road the sumac was the color of raspberry jelly.

Mrs. Fish was waiting on the street for us. Boxes were piled up on the sidewalk. "All that stuff coming?" Old Dad said

"And lots more." Mrs. Fish said cheerfully.

We carried down tables and chairs, boxes, bundles, bags, and plants. Greta and William came down, Toot Sweet in his cage and finally Face Pole. Chairs were lashed to the top of the car, a laundry bag bulged from a window, and Greta and William sat on top of everything in the back seat. The pickup truck was crammed full, too, from top to bottom. Old Dad and I drove home slowly, with Mrs. Fish following in her car.

At the house, out came everything—the boxes and bundles, the bags and plants, the canary cage and William's bed. Face Pole went up against the side of the house, Mrs. Fish's wooden wind chimes above our front door, rag rugs down on the floor. As fast as we emptied a box, another took its place. The shelves were all filled, the pegs on the wall were overflowing, and the bed was piled high with sheets and blankets, towels and tablecloths. I thought we would never get everything put away, but somehow we did. Mrs. Fish found places for everything.

It was late when we finished. We ate bread and tuna fish and milk, sitting around the table. It was just plain, not like the fancy suppers I had dreamed about, but it was so good. It was almost like Mrs. Fish had always lived with us.

The next day Old Dad went to work in the dump as usual. Mrs. Fish went to her job, and I went to school. "Off to the workaday world, dear ones," Mrs. Fish said. "See you tonight."

Everything was the same—the school bus, the kids, my class—but everything was different. I felt as if sparks were flying off me. I felt light, as if I were hardly walking on the floors, as if I could do anything.

And when I walked into the lunchroom and saw Lacey sitting at a table with an empty seat next to her, it was just as if it had been planned. *That seat was for me.*

I walked between the tables. I had a shivery feeling inside. I was going to do it. I was going to sit down next to her. But I was scared. What if she snubbed me? I stopped. *Do it, dear one. If you don't try, you'll never know.* I could almost hear Mrs. Fish talking to me.

I sat down. Lacey looked over at me. "Hello," I said.

"Hello," she said.

Then we just looked at each other.

I took a deep breath. "Same old Swiss cheese," I said, taking out my sandwich. "Want a bite?"